High Performance Habits
Making Success a Habit

Scott F. Paradis

http://Success101Workshop.com

Books by
Scott F. Paradis:

High Performance Habits
Making Success a Habit

How to Succeed at Anything
In 3 Simple Steps

Success 101 How Life Works
Know the Rules, Play to Win

*Warriors Diplomats Heroes
Why America's Army Succeeds*
Lessons for Business and Life

Promise and Potential
A Life of Wisdom, Courage, Strength, and Will

And coming soon:

High Performance Health and Fitness
MNOP Habits: Mindset, Nutrition, get Out and Play

Money
The New Science of Making It

Build Me A Son
A story of Hope, Love and Renewal

Are You Really Better Than Average?
Where You Stand and the Fastest Way to the Top

Change your life with these online courses and workshops by
Scott F. Paradis:

High Performance Habits
Making Success a Habit
www.Success101Habits.com

Success 101 How to Succeed
Focus on Fundamentals
www.Success101Succeed.com

High Performance Health and Fitness
MNOP Habits: Mindset, Nutrition, get Out and Play
www.Success101Health.com

Money
The New Science of Making It
www.Success101Money.com

Success 101 How Life Works
Know the Rules, Play to Win

High Performance Leadership
Fundamental Leadership Habits

Loving 101
Making Love a Habit

Achievement Theology
Bringing the Wisdom of the Ages to Life

High Performance Habits
Making Success a Habit

Copyright © 2014 Scott F. Paradis
All rights reserved

The information presented herein represents the views of the author. These views may change. While every attempt has been made to verify the information in this book, the author does not assume any responsibility for errors, inaccuracies, or omissions.

Published and distributed by:

Cornerstone Achievements
New Hampshire and Virginia, USA
www.cornerstone-achievements.com

ISBN: 978-0-9798638-3-7 (soft cover and e-reader)

Published in the United States of America.

This book is dedicated to those who raise the bar by adopting high performance habits. These are men and women who embrace life exploring and experiencing, creating and contributing; they express more life. You can be one of them.

This book is dedicated to you.

Table of Contents

Preface – 1

Foreword – 3

Chapter 1 Soar like an Eagle – 7

Part 1: A Few Simple Things

Chapter 2 Going the Extra Mile – 21

Chapter 3 Build on a Solid Foundation – 29

Chapter 4 The Vital Few and Trivial Many – 41

Chapter 5 What Is a Habit? – 49

Part 2: High Performance Habits

Chapter 6 Every Attempt a Learning Opportunity – 63

Chapter 7 The Right Habits – 69

Chapter 8 Attitude and Mindset – 79

Chapter 9 Make an Impression – 87

Part 3: You are Not Alone

Chapter 10 Relationships Make or Break – 99

Chapter 11 It's All About Relationships – 105

Chapter 12 Are We Communicating? – 113

Chapter 13 Running with the Right Crowd – 123

Part 4: Making Success a Habit

Chapter 14 Walk by Faith – 135

Chapter 15 Cultivating Habits – 141

Chapter 16 Overcoming What Holds Us Back – 151

Chapter 17 Leading by Example – 159

Chapter 18 Change Your Habits, Change Your Life – 169

Table of Contents (continued)

Chapter 19 Take the Next Step – 177

Afterword – 183

Appendix A: High Performance Habits Summary List – 185

Appendix B: High Performance Habits Change Process / Change Plan – 187

Appendix C: Feedback Request & Contact Info – 192

About the Author – 194

Acknowledgements – 196

About Success 101 Workshop – 197

HIGH PERFORMANCE HABITS

Preface

The difference between the super successful, the high achievers and all the rest is not looks or talent, intelligence or education, status or wealth. These trappings of success are the byproduct of something else: habits; high performance habits. The super successful don't have access to a secret or possess some magical ingredient others lack. High achievers make the process of succeeding a routine. The super successful employ habits that produce extraordinary results. *High Performance Habits* focuses on those habits.

In *High Performance Habits* you will discover what it takes, both the little measures and the extreme efforts, to move away from an ordinary life and begin to live an extraordinary life. By changing a few key routines you can make success a habit. With new habits the circumstances of your life will begin to change and you will enjoy an entirely new experience. Are you ready for a change? Are you ready for a challenge?

High Performance Habits examines the components of a complete life: everything from health to wealth to work to relationships to ferret out the mindset, the focus and the behaviors that really matter. We will make sense of why some people, with apparently every advantage, struggle and fail while others, facing seemingly insurmountable obstacles, succeed wildly.

By the end of *High Performance Habits* you will come to realize:

HIGH PERFORMANCE HABITS

Success is a choice, a choice you make. You *CAN* make success a habit!

This book, though not exactly word for word, is practically a transcript of an audio-video course published online titled: **High Performance Habits, Making Success a Habit** offered by Scott F. Paradis. Look for this course and others by Scott F. Paradis on the World Wide Web.

And finally a note about style. You'll notice immediately this book is not written to conform to AP style. My approach is informal, you might say, conversational. Some sentences begin with *ands* and *buts* and end with prepositions. My intent is to communicate with you as effectively and directly as possible. Please forgive my lack of elegance as I hope you connect with the truths the words are meant to convey.

HIGH PERFORMANCE HABITS

Foreword

By reading ***High Performance Habits*** you are embarking on a journey, a transformative journey. This book is intended to move you through a process of sorts. This transformation process begins with words on a page (or symbols on a digital reader) and hopefully advances through personal reflection and engaging exercises to bring you to a new, better, more fulfilling place. If you commit to the work, the self-development, you will engage in some detective work and conduct some introspection. You will dissect the habit cycle and you will determine which habits are driving your train and specifically which habits you must change to set yourself on a new course.

You will initiate and complete a habits change process working through these steps:

1. Conduct a ***Personal Habits Inventory***.
2. Review the ***High Performance Habits Summary*** and compare your habits to these.
3. Compile and assess an ***Associates Inventory.***
4. Compile and assess your group ***Cultural Habits Inventories.***
5. Evaluate your habits and produce a ***Habits Change Plan.***
6. ***Execute a habits change process*** (implement your plan).
7. ***Assess your progress, update and revise your plan*** (prepare to change your next habit) ***and execute a habits change process again. Repeat as necessary.***

HIGH PERFORMANCE HABITS

My only request is that you open yourself to the process. Be willing to take risks. And for best results, do more than is required. Go the extra mile. Look over the next hill. Continue taking the next step and keep moving forward. There is no other way to go.

Embrace the adventure, change your habits. Develop new high performance habits. You will build your faith and quite possibly surprise yourself when you begin to see what you are truly capable of accomplishing.

To help you progress enlist the support of positive, growth-oriented, supportive people. No one succeeds alone. I'm here for you, but there is some distance between us. Surround yourself with loving people, people who are going somewhere, people who are embracing life and you won't help but succeed. **You are not alone, you are loved; there is nothing to fear; and all things are possible! Now get on with making success a habit.**

*All things are possible
For one who believes.*

HIGH PERFORMANCE HABITS

Chapter 1
Soar like an Eagle

What is the difference between the high fliers, the wealthy, the connected, the accomplished and all the rest?

Is it looks and talent; intelligence and education; access, environment or opportunity?

Why do some people get all the attention and seem to bask in the spotlight, while other, equally capable people struggle just to get noticed?

Why do a select few earn extraordinary amounts of money and accumulate property and possessions, wealth of all kinds, while most spend their days laboring to make the house payment, the car payment, the student loan payment, and the credit card payment? These laborers long for the fast approach of Friday.

How is it some people establish and maintain loving, supportive relationships that last a lifetime – they have trusted confidantes, loyal friends and committed allies they can rely on, while most deal with the drama of off-again, on-again relationships and needy, demanding family members and dare I say, friends?

How do some people demonstrate truly exceptional feats of physical prowess and possess skills and abilities seemingly beyond the reach of commoners, while most relegate athletic pursuits to lifting a beer and cheering others efforts from the stands or the couch?

Chapter 1: Soar like an Eagle

How is it that some people just perform at a high level and reap the rewards, while most settle for, and settle into mediocrity?

Are you one of those high-performers?

Would you like to be?

I suspect you were moved to pick up this book by one of three motives. First, and hopefully, a desire to have more, do more and become more. You may have been moved by a desire to validate what you already recognize as exceptional potential. Or you may be viewing this out of curiosity. You want to look behind the curtain and see if the shiny, glowing object might be a treasure; something valuable, useful and helpful.

Well, welcome to ***High Performance Habits***; a program to make success a habit.

Conventional wisdom tells us the well-worn path to achievement is through the sometimes delightful, sometimes mystifying, always rewarding wilderness of education and hard work. But knowing that path exists, the path of education and hard work, does not, in and of itself provide a satisfactory route to high achievement. There is more to it than that.

You know this to be true. You know highly educated people who lack common sense; who can't seem to get ahead; who struggle like the rest, perhaps more so. You

Chapter 1: Soar like an Eagle

know hard workers, people who give it their all and are just treading water; struggling to get by.

It's more than education and hard work. And that's what **High Performance Habits** is all about; making a leap; doing something different. **High Performance Habits** is about making success a habit.

Have you heard about the eagle raised by the prairie chickens?

A pair of mighty eagles built their nest high up on a rocky cliff. Three eggs lay in the nest when one night a terrible storm blew through. Winds battered that nest. Flying debris shook one of the eggs free. That egg rolled out of the nest and off the rocky outcropping. As luck would have it, the egg did not break, it rolled and fell and dropped all the way down that cliff until it landed amongst a family of prairie chickens.

That eagle was born amongst chickens. He was an odd looking chick but the mother hen accepted him and taught that eagle the prairie chicken way of life. That eagle grew up pecking the ground and hopping around searching for measly scraps; mostly grubs and other insects.

As he grew, the eagle recognized he wasn't like the prairie chickens, but he didn't know where he fit in, or what he could do. With his sharp eyes he spied some majestic birds high overhead. That young eagle marveled at those

Chapter 1: Soar like an Eagle

birds in flight. He longed to soar like those regal creatures, but the chickens were busy everyday scratching in the dirt. So the eagle assumed his place among the chickens.

Years went by. That eagle clawed and scratched out a meager existence, but he always had a sharp eye turned to the sky. His very being yearned to express something, something our eagle could not fathom. He knew something wasn't quite right, but he had no example to follow, no other way to go.

Finally our eagle grew old and weary. He lived a lifetime among the chickens. He had scratched and clawed and scratched and clawed some more. While he kicked up dust his entire life he envied those stately beings that sailed the breezes high above the cliffs. He longed to do what they could do, to have what they have, to be what they were.

If only he knew.

The tragedy is, that eagle had all the tools he needed to live a different life. He could have flown, he could have soared, he could have been so much more, but he didn't know how; he had no one to show him the way.

He had the talent, the ability, even the desire; he just never saw the opportunity. That eagle lived his entire life in the dust and the dirt, with the chickens. He never fulfilled his potential. He never spread his wings and soared. He never assumed his place amongst the eagles.

What about you?

Chapter 1: Soar like an Eagle

You recognize high achievers; we all do. We see them around us; making things happen. We secretly, or maybe not so secretly, aspire to be like them.

We just aren't quite sure what they have that we don't. Surely that have talents we lack. Surely they have connections we don't. Surely they have resources we don't have access to. How else could they be moving so much faster than we are? How else could they be traveling so much farther than we are? How else can they be achieving so much more than we are?

They are making success a habit.

Well, I'm here to tell you; you can make success a habit too.

You are an eagle. You have talents and abilities you have not yet tapped. You are capable of so much more.

In **High Performance Habits** we're going to take a journey, a journey of discovery. We are going to examine what separates the high achievers from all the rest. And we're going to learn the habits that really make the difference.

You see, achievement, success in life, is not a matter of luck or chance or fate. It doesn't come down to looks and talent, intelligence and education, access, environment and opportunity. You have the ability to influence all these.

Chapter 1: Soar like an Eagle

What separates high performers from all the rest is the focus and effort they put in to developing habits that set them on the fast-track, the sure path to success.

In ***High Performance Habits*** you are going to learn what it takes to move from average to exceptional, from envious to accomplished, from mediocrity to mastery. It comes down to understanding and executing a few fundamentals. Success comes down to adopting high performance habits.

Now let's be clear.

What we are undertaking, what we are attempting is in fact simple. But this is the point I must stress: it's not easy. To change, to change direction, to get new results, new experiences in your life; to grow and become a new accomplished, high performer is going to take effort. Remember our conventional wisdom. If being a high performer were easy, don't you think everyone would be a high performer?

Sure they would, but it's not easy. Changing your habits, changing your beliefs; changing your life; is going to take some effort. It's going to mean some discomfort and some pain.

If you are looking for the easy answer, it's not here.

Yes, you've discovered the shortcut, the solution to your problems, but I don't want you to entertain any illusions. Making success a habit is going to take work, painstaking work. Work you can do. Work you will enjoy, at least

Chapter 1: Soar like an Eagle

sometimes. This change we're suggesting is easily within your ability. You have the potential for greatness within you. You just have to want it enough.

If you want it enough; if you want to be a high performer, if you want to live an exceptional life, then you can learn to believe. And once you believe, anything is possible.

So, resolve, here and now, to endure the discomfort, to embrace the pain of resistance and the anxiety of overcoming your fear. Let's start making success a habit.

So, where are we going to go?

High Performance Habits is presented in four parts or sections.

The first part is intended to build a foundation. We're going set the stage by covering the big picture. The first section introduces and explains the basics, the fundamentals. Here you are going to take an inventory of the habits that have made your life.

The second and third sections focus more directly on the habits high performers develop and nurture to achieve success.

The fourth and final section is where the challenging work begins. We are going to go through the process of changing habits that don't serve you into habits that do serve you. You are going to have to invest time and energy to take control of your life. It's here that you are going to begin

Chapter 1: Soar like an Eagle

remaking yourself into the exceptional person I know you are; it's just a matter of choosing and developing the right habits.

It really is as simple as that.

Before we jump in; or if you're still questioning the value of moving forward with **High Performance Habits** at all, let's consider a few objective measures of high achievement; how we recognize high performers.

High performers simply excel in one or more dimensions of life. They create or contribute and by so doing distinguish themselves from the masses. These dimensions of achievement are: the physical, the mental, the social, the spiritual and or the material. Now, many of these dimensions are difficult to measure. But, when it gets down to it, what we're all after is happiness. We want our lives to be full and fulfilling and we want to be happy.

If you took my **Success 101 How to Succeed** course or read the book or some of my other works, you are familiar with where I'm coming from. Suffice it to say, for our purposes here; high performers organize and conduct their lives in a way, using habits, to outperform most people. It's not that they are fundamentally more talented, more creative, and more capable than others. It's that they use the power of habit to keep them on track and moving forward to ever higher achievement.

Chapter 1: Soar like an Eagle

How do we distinguish a high performer?

We can't observe all the traits that set high performers apart. They are not necessarily easy to measure, but here are a few obvious ones:

They are always growing and learning; challenging themselves;

They perform athletically and consistently win;

They lead effectively;

They are centered, self-aware and self-assured; confident;

They nurture and support people; others are naturally drawn to them;

They build organizations that add value;

And they control resources and amass material wealth.

Not all high performers are exceptional athletes, or exceptional intellects, or amass wealth. And, by the way, not everyone who is famous or wealthy is a high-performer. But let's consider a few observable measures to better determine who the high performers are.

We all naturally have a self-serving bias. Besides protecting our body we are engaged twenty-four seven in protecting our psyches from anything that might threaten our self-esteem. Usually, mostly, but not always people tend to have an inflated view of themselves.

Chapter 1: Soar like an Eagle

Most will tell you they are better than average drivers. Many believe they are more intelligent than most; that they are harder working; that they are more talented and capable than most.

For those feigning confidence, confronting the brutal facts usually offers a humbling realization. Most people avoid confronting the facts however. These people prefer to keep alive a self-made fantasy despite the truths the world around them reveals.

Are you willing to consider the facts?

Here are a few measures to get us started.

Let's get physical.

Two thirds of American adults are overweight or obese.

How close are you to your ideal weight? High performers, people who have it together across all dimensions of life, are fit and near their ideal weight.

Do you set aside time routinely, perhaps daily to read and study, to learn and grow? High performers actively work to develop themselves intellectually and expand their expertise.

How are your relationships?

High performers associate with and surround themselves with positive, like-minded people. High performers lead by

Chapter 1: Soar like an Eagle

example but know that this journey of life is not taken solo; relationships are important. High performers work diligently at connecting with other people; and not just superficially, but genuinely.

How is your anxiety or stress level?

High performers get stressed, we all do. High performers just know enough about themselves, this world and their place in it to realize that they must take direct measures, across multiple dimensions, to mitigate stress and stay centered.

And finally, how about the material realm, are you wealthy?

We can see high performers create, contribute and collect. They earn more than most and many control vast wealth.

The median household income in the United States is about fifty thousand dollars a year. Are you making at least that much? To be in the top ten percent of households in the United States members of your household have to be bringing in more than one hundred and fourteen thousand dollars a year.

To be in the top ten percent of individual earners you have to be making at least forty-four dollars per hour or roughly ninety thousand dollars annually. How do you stack up?

Chapter 1: Soar like an Eagle

What about the wealth you've been able to accumulate. The average American household has a net worth of around seventy-five thousand dollars. Households in the top ten percent have net worth on the order of one million dollars.

By objective measures of health and fitness; positive, supportive relationships; and earnings and wealth, are you a high performer?

You can be.

Learn the habits that allow average people, people like you and me, to achieve exceptional results.

Your life can truly be remarkable. All you have to do is learn and then adopt high performance habits and make success a habit.

Let's get to work. Shall we?

Part 1

A Few Simple Things

HIGH PERFORMANCE HABITS

Chapter 2
Going the Extra Mile

Out of the night that covers me,
Black as the pit from pole to pole,
I thank whatever gods may be
For my unconquerable soul.

In the fell clutch of circumstance
I have not winced nor cried aloud.
Under the bludgeonings of chance
My head is bloody, but unbowed.

Beyond this place of wrath and tears
Looms but the horror of the shade,
And yet the menace of the years
Finds, and shall find me unafraid.

It matters not how strait the gate,
How charged with punishments the scroll,
I am the master of my fate:
I am the captain of my soul.

Invictus by William Earnest Henley

Andrew Carnegie was master of his fate; was captain of his soul. He was a man who lived a true life rags to riches

Chapter 2: Going the Extra Mile

story. Andrew Carnegie made his way by going the extra mile.

After the textile mills had essentially forced Andrew's father out of business as a handloom weaver the Carnegie family had to borrow money to emigrate from Scotland to the United States.

Andrew's first job in America at the age of 13 in 1848 was as a bobbin boy, changing spools of thread 12 hours a day, six days a week in a Pittsburgh, Pennsylvania cotton factory. His starting wage: $1.20 per week. Now, I'm no relation to Andrew Carnegie, but my grandfather started out the same way. He worked as a bobbin boy in the mills of Lawrence and Lowell, Massachusetts as a young immigrant boy from Quebec, Canada. I could see the bends in his fingers, deformed by the tedious and difficult task of fitting spools of thread for hours on end. My grandfather, though a remarkable man in his own right never went on to build an empire like Andrew Carnegie did.

From humble beginnings Andrew Carnegie went on to become the richest man in the world; the Prince of Steel.

When he was in his early 30's, after he had amassed a small fortune, Carnegie wrote this to himself:

> *Man does not live by bread alone. I have known millionaires starving for lack, and I know workmen, and so-called poor men, who revel in luxuries beyond the power of millionaires to reach. It is the mind that makes the body rich. There is no class as*

Chapter 2: Going the Extra Mile

wretched as that which possesses money and nothing else. Money can only be the useful drudge of things immeasurably higher than itself.

Now some will look at Carnegie's life and say 'he was lucky'. Well luck favors the bold and the prepared. In truth luck has nothing to do with life's outcomes. Everything serves a purpose. Andrew Carnegie faced some decisions, he made some choices, he charted his own course.

Being ambitious, young Andrew kept an eye out for opportunities beyond that textile factory. He soon found a job as a telegraph messenger, doubling his salary.

Andrew was a very hard worker. He would memorize all of the locations of Pittsburgh's businesses and the faces of important men. With this knowledge he became the fastest and most reliable messenger in his station. In addition to excelling at his job, being a messenger allowed young Andrew to begin making key connections with the movers and shakers in Pittsburg.

On and off the job Andrew was focused, focused on bettering himself and his family. Paying close attention to the telegraph he quickly learned to distinguish the differing sounds the incoming signals produced. He developed the ability to translate signals by ear, without having to write them down and within a year was promoted to telegraph operator.

In his off time Carnegie's education and passion for reading were greatly assisted by a local man who opened his

Chapter 2: Going the Extra Mile

personal library to working boys each Saturday night. Carnegie was a consistent borrower and a "self-made man" in his personal, professional and cultural development. His intellectual capacity, his willingness to work hard, his perseverance, and his alertness brought further opportunities.

In 1853, Carnegie took a job at the Pennsylvania Railroad as a secretary and telegraph operator at a salary of $4.00 per week. Then, at only age eighteen, Carnegie began a rapid advance through the company. He was at the right place at the right time and he allied with the right people. He was at the cutting edge of a massive new technology; railroads were expanding rapidly; and he was working for one of largest organizations in America. Carnegie cut his teeth in business with the Pennsylvania Railroad ultimately becoming the superintendent of the Pittsburgh Division.

At the age of twenty Andrew's father died. This forced young Carnegie to become the primary provider for himself, his mother and his younger brother. Fortunately to this point in his working life Andrew had carefully honed important habits that would serve him well throughout his career. He was a voracious learner, always improving himself; he never shied away from hard work, constantly going the extra mile; and he realized the importance of association, he connected with people who were capable and ambitious at all levels of society.

The most profound life lesson he learned though came from his years in poverty and at times of struggle and strife. He developed a habit of spirit that served him through the trials of life. He discovered that the cause of success is not

Chapter 2: Going the Extra Mile

something apart from the individual; rather it is a force so intangible the majority of people never recognize it. He termed this cause a force he labeled the **other self.**

The 'other self' makes itself known and exerts an influence when failure strikes and the individual is obliged through adversity and temporary defeat to change his or her habits and actually think their way out of difficulty. Carnegie came to realize that failure was nothing more than an opportunity to reevaluate and reenergize yourself with a new plan or purpose.

Most real failures, Carnegie said, are due to limits people set in their own minds. If they have the courage to go one step further, they will discover the error. Listen to your other self; it will guide you in times of distress.

Carnegie believed in the power of spirit and the supremacy of mind. As a wealthy man he made it his purpose, 'To contribute to the enlightenment and the joys of the mind, to the things of the spirit, to all that tends to bring into the lives of toilers sweetness and light.'

Through his associations at the railroad company Carnegie was guided into some extremely lucrative investments. He did have to take some risks however. He ended up putting his mother's house up as collateral for one investment. The risk paid off. Eventually Carnegie was able to compound his investment earnings in railroad related ventures, railcars, iron, bridges and so on, and oil into a tidy sum. He left his salaried position at the age of 30.

Chapter 2: Going the Extra Mile

What Carnegie did in the 1850's and 60's was like compounding investments in Microsoft and Apple, Amazon and Net Flix, and Google and Twitter today. He surveyed the business environment and made choices that brought him an immense fortune.

In addition to the knowledge and experience he garnered in the railroad business Carnegie accumulated capital and fostered associations and partnerships everywhere he could. He pursued opportunities as they arose.

After the Civil War, seeing opportunities in recovery, increasing industrial growth and westward expansion, Carnegie started a bridge company and iron works in Pittsburg. He vertically integrated his operations owning everything from raw materials to transportation to refining and distribution.

Given the immensity of his operations he still believed in the uncompromising power of people. He claimed that if you took all the stuff away, the coal, the rail lines and the factories, leaving him with his people he could rebuild it all in four years. Carnegie recognized success is all about relationships, it's all about people.

By the late 1880's Carnegie was the largest steel manufacturer in the world.

With his eyes turned to philanthropic interests in 1901 Carnegie sold his entire steel holdings. J.P. Morgan brokered a deal for Carnegie's steel empire to form what became U.S. Steel. Carnegie devoted the remainder of his life to giving his fortune away.

Chapter 2: Going the Extra Mile

Carnegie was born poor, became the richest man in the world, and died a preeminent philanthropist. He believed the world was in need of a practical, understandable philosophy of achievement. A philosophy organized from factual knowledge gained from the experience of men and women in the great university of life. He felt that philosophy of achievement should be taught in schools and colleges across the country and around the world.

Carnegie believed people were capable but had much to learn, so he devoted himself to helping those who were willing to help themselves.

He endowed over 20 institutions and organizations in the fields of research, education, music and the arts, and in pursuit of world peace.

He established nearly 3,000 libraries across the United States and around the world.

Carnegie held, "...the man who dies rich dies disgraced." He said, the wealthy are stewards of treasure. They must administer their fortunes for the good of mankind.

Before his death in 1919, Andrew Carnegie donated over 350 million dollars (about $5 billion in modern terms) for various causes. He concluded his life having successfully executed his dictum:

- To spend the first third of one's life getting all the education one can.
- To spend the next third making all the money one can.

Chapter 2: Going the Extra Mile

- To spend the last third giving it all away for worthwhile causes.

Andrew Carnegie was master of his fate, captain of his soul. He developed the habit of going the extra mile in all aspects of his life. His influence is still felt to this day.

Chapter 3
Build on a Solid Foundation

Andrew Carnegie lived an extraordinary life.

Some say he was lucky. There's no such thing. Others say he had advantages. He came to America without a penny to his name. Others say he had natural gifts and talents which set him apart.

You know what?

You have natural gifts and talents. You have unfettered access to energy and motivation and power.

Andrew Carnegie was a remarkable individual; a man who lived an extraordinary life.

The truth is you too are a remarkable individual and you too can live an extraordinary life. You just have to start doing things a certain way; a way that leads to success. To do those things that lead to success you must build your life on a solid foundation and become a successful person.

Developing the right habits will make you a successful person. Developing the right habits will ensure your life rests on a solid foundation.

In *High Performance Habits* we focus on habits. We'll discuss the habit cycle in an upcoming chapter, but first here we have to cover the fundamentals. We've got to start with the foundation. The foundation is the most important part of

Chapter 3: Build on a Solid Foundation

any structure. Your foundation is the most important part of your life.

You see results, what manifests as our experience, are a product of who we are. The world around us, the circumstances of our environment and the situations we get ourselves into are not indiscriminately thrust upon us. That world out there is a reflection of what's within us; what's inside us. What we experience in life is an expression of who we are. Each new circumstance is a revelation of where we **intend** to go, of what we **intend** to experience, of who we **intend** to become.

Where does this awesome potential come from?

From the *Source*.

Life is an expression of how well we are connected to the *Source*; the source of unlimited energy, motivation, talent and power.

The *Source* is limitless and universally accessible. Our connection to the *Source* is our foundation for this life.

Let me ask you; when you go on a road trip do you prefer to drive, ride shotgun or do you prefer to sit in the back with no control and no responsibility?

You see, in life you can drive, you can ride shotgun and navigate, or you can sit in the back and go along for the ride.

Now we all know backseat drivers; they whine and complain an awful lot but they don't have any responsibility so they get what they get.

Chapter 3: Build on a Solid Foundation

Life is a journey. There is no sitting still. You're on the road trip. You get to pick your position: driver, shotgun, disinterested passenger. You can even change positions along the highway. You have the ability. The choice is yours. Make the smart choice.

So what matters on a road trip, on your road trip?

Where you're going; how far and by what route, and how fast you travel.

Your road trip depends on your foundation; your connection to the *Source*.

You see, life rests on a foundation; a foundation of energy and intelligence. How grounded you are, how solid and well-built your foundation is, how connected you are, makes all the difference.

This connection to the *Source* can be determined by how you answer three questions. Now, how you answer these questions is not by way of your intellect. You can quickly offer or immediately rationalize answers to these questions as soon as you read them. The real answers to these questions however, are not determined by your intellect. The real answers to these questions are determined by how you live your life and what you experience.

The questions are:

First, is this world a safe and welcoming or a dangerous and unwelcoming place?

Chapter 3: Build on a Solid Foundation

Second, are you connected, capable and confident or not?

And finally, do you have a place in the world, a purpose, a reason for being?

Our connection to the *Source*, our foundation, is reflected in our beliefs about the nature of this reality, this world; our beliefs about ourselves; and our beliefs about our place in this world.

If we have a solid connection, if our life is built on a strong foundation, we are positive and motivated. We have a reason for being, a purpose. We are engaged in the adventure.

A solid foundation means all systems are go. We usually, mostly feel good and are healthy. From that grounding, from the footing of a solid foundation, we build and maintain a network of support. Other people, relationships, are a central element of the formation and long term viability of our connection to the *Source*, our foundation.

Life springs from a universal source. We build our lives upon and our success is determined by our connection to the *Source*. This connection is our foundation.

A strong foundation allows us good health; we get to travel in a fully functioning, highly capable vehicle.

Positive, supportive relationships reinforce our connection to the *Source*. Upon this base we build our lives. Upon this base, all the trappings of life manifest. Our core beliefs are what connect us to the *Source*.

Chapter 3: Build on a Solid Foundation

It's not that anyone has more or less access to the blessings of the *Source*; it comes down to if we **believe** we do. From the *Source* achievement, wealth, success; happiness spring forth.

An illustration here may help explain this point.

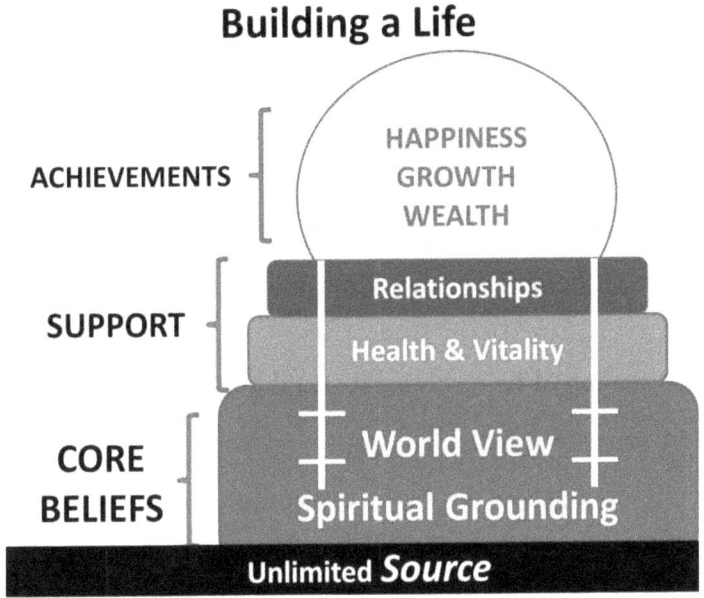

Play an imagination game with me right now.

Imagine for a moment human beings coming off an assembly line. These beings have immense abilities. Each and every one is extremely capable, extremely talented, and extremely gifted. Each one has the capacity for greatness, the skill to soar to great heights, to contribute and create.

Chapter 3: Build on a Solid Foundation

Each human being has access to supernatural power and divine wisdom. Everyone has truly awesome potential.

Now what is one of the last stations on an assembly line? It's that station that sets the default; the standard operating setting.

We have awesome beings, capable of extraordinary exploits. What would you set the default to?

You'd set the default for maximum performance. Each being naturally and automatically has the ability to manifest awe-inspiring potential. Why not set them for maximum performance?

Set on default, people come into the world empowered with:

A feeling of being connected and loved;

A sense of safety and security;

The realization they have some autonomy and the ability to create;

And the wisdom and insight to grow to overcome any obstacle they face while engaged in the adventure.

These people, set on maximum performance would fully embrace the adventure. With unfettered access to unlimited talent and power these people would do amazing things. They would live exceptional lives. They would explore and create, connect and contribute.

Are you imagining?

Chapter 3: Build on a Solid Foundation

These would be high performing people.

Now back to reality.

We have people with awesome potential. But, too often what do we get?

Instead of embracing the adventure and experiencing a full and fulfilling life, something happens to our default setting. We come into this world and immediately we feel the weight of resistance and fear.

The switch begins to be thrown. The switches begin being turned from maximum performance to some base, some ground setting.

Instead of tremendous feats of daring and creativity we close down, we hide, we settle. We let fear rule our lives.

The default setting of high potential and high performance becomes a setting focused on surviving; just getting by.

Because of what we face, the weight of the world and the limitations of our bodies and the examples of those who care for and surround us, we determine we are in a dangerous place. We had better not go too far or move too fast. And what traits do we manifest in this threatening, dangerous world?

We strive for immediate gratification and we maintain a short-term focus. Everything could be lost if we don't get it now.

Chapter 3: Build on a Solid Foundation

We avoid risk. We'd rather conform and follow than strike out on our own path. We can't risk losing whatever we have.

We work to satisfy our selves rather than to contribute to the greater good. We justify our selfishness as we have determined life to be one big competition and I have to get mine.

We sit in the backseat awash in negative emotions, judging, condemning, criticizing and complaining. We never take responsibility. We never fulfill our potential.

We invest our time and energy protecting our bodies and our self-esteem. We must be right; we must be certain; and we much prefer that things don't change.

How is it we go from such extraordinary potential, remember our extraordinary beings on the assembly line, to such mediocre performance?

Our default is set to maximum, to optimum, to extreme potential and virtually from the get go, from birth, we start dialing it back.

Life grabs hold of us and we start kicking back the switch.

The weight of the world impacts our psyches and the examples of the people around us influence the formation of our core beliefs.

Chapter 3: Build on a Solid Foundation

So instead of living as high performers; as eagles, people who aspire to do great things and who actually do great things; we determine to get by. We settle for good enough.

Our core beliefs, what our lives are built on, determine our habits of mind and action, and our habits are what primarily move us forward.

We need to start throwing the switches back to the default setting. We need to start driving, or at least navigating, and set ourselves on the right course; the course to high achievement and happiness.

People who are not realizing their potential have come to believe they are separate and alone in a dangerous world. These core beliefs become habits of feeling, thinking and acting.

The results that manifest in life are an expression of who we **believe** ourselves to be.

Change the beliefs and the habits change.

However, **changing core beliefs is not so easy**.

So, here in *High Performance Habits* we are going to pursue a different strategy. We are going to change our habits to change our beliefs.

In *High Performance Habits* we intentionally work from the outside in. To instill in ourselves high performance habits we have to change our core beliefs: our beliefs about

Chapter 3: Build on a Solid Foundation

this reality, about ourselves and our capabilities, and about our place in this world. But, changing core beliefs is a hard nut to crack.

In the very last chapter of *High Performance Habits* we're going to discuss the habit ladder. This is a strategy for making small changes that ultimately initiate big changes that last. We'll get there in due time, but for now let's start where we are.

We, you and I, have unlimited potential. To expose that potential, to activate it, we just have to believe that we already have unlimited potential. It's already there. We have access to an unimaginable array of gifts, talents; possibilities waiting expression. You can have more, do more and become more. Yes you can!

Everything we are, everything we do, and everything that manifests in our experience rests on, is interpreted by, and resonates from, our core beliefs. And core beliefs are built over time.

So rather than attempt to move the big gear all at once, directly; that is change core beliefs about the world, ourselves and our place in it; those drivers of life habits; we are going to make small changes to nurture our beliefs, to build faith incrementally.

With small victories we cultivate that growing seed of faith. With some determined effort we **can** change our core beliefs and put ourselves on a new path.

Chapter 3: Build on a Solid Foundation

Changing habits takes effort. We've got work to do.

Let's lay our cards out on the table.

We've got to be clear about a couple of things.

First: life is not a matter of fate, luck or chance. The controls are in our hands. We must believe how we feel, the choices we make, and the things we do matter. Our journey through life is not up to whims of circumstance. You are in fact captain of your soul, master of your fate.

Second: life, this reality, by design has a purpose. That purpose is for us to grow and express more life.

Circumstances, obstacles and challenges are a fact of life and serve a purpose; to advance our cause. Never concede to a challenge or obstacle. You can choose another course, but stopping, sitting and sulking as many people do, some for years, decades even, does not move you toward your goal.

Some people wallow in despair or indecision the majority of their lives. Don't waste your life that way.

Encumbrances, obstacles, challenges are circumstances to use to change who we are. Changing who we are inside changes what we experience outside.

Sounds easy enough.

We've certainly got some challenges to overcome.

We've got some growing to do.

Chapter 3: Build on a Solid Foundation

So let's start by focusing on the levers; those few key things that matter most. I'll explain what I mean in the next chapter.

Chapter 4
The Vital Few and Trivial Many

Did you ever notice that about twenty percent of criminals commit eighty percent of crimes? Or that twenty percent of motorists cause eighty percent of accidents?

Have you realized about twenty percent of streets back up with eighty percent of the traffic? It's probably the same twenty percent you are usually on.

And have you realized about twenty percent of clients or customers typically account for eighty percent of profits or problems?

Look around your home, look at the wear and tear on your carpets. About twenty percent of your carpet gets eighty percent of the wear and tear.

And how about this: have you noticed that you wear about twenty percent of your clothes eighty percent of the time?

Be honest now; I know we all have favorites.

There exists an inherent imbalance between causes and results, inputs and outputs, effort and reward. Some inputs produce little output while other causes produce extraordinary results. This imbalance is known as the *Pareto Principle* or more commonly as the *80/20 Rule*.

Chapter 4: The Vital Few and Trivial Many

The *Pareto Principle* states that eighty percent of results in business and in life stem from a mere twenty percent of efforts. Basically some things matter more; some few things produce outsized results.

Habits are actions we take consistently, automatically. Their effect is cumulative over time, for good or bad. Our habits are among those things that produce outsized results.

The *80/20 Rule* stipulates causes or inputs come in two varieties: first the majority category, these are causes with little impact – the eighty percent – then there is the second or minority category, these are the causes or inputs with major or dominant impact – twenty percent causes.

If we want to be high performers, if we want to achieve exceptional results in life, we have to focus on that second category: causes or inputs with dominant or outsized impact.

To be most successful focus your efforts, your time, energy and talents, on things that matter; on things that produce big results; on developing high performance habits.

Vilfredo Frederico Damaso Pareto lived from 1848 to 1923. He was an Italian engineer, sociologist, economist, political scientist, and philosopher. He began his professional career as a civil engineer, but he had broad interests. He went on to be a professor at universities in Italy and then Switzerland.

During his exploration into the fields of sociology and economics Pareto noticed a particular pattern of disparity as

Chapter 4: The Vital Few and Trivial Many

to who controlled the majority of wealth. Over time he examined all the property records he could get his hands on and discovered that about twenty percent of the people always control about eighty percent of the wealth. This pattern held true for every location and time in history he could compare. Pareto discovered income followed a power law probability distribution; this 80-20 ratio. Other researchers went on to verify this ratio holds across a wide spectrum of observations.

It is critical that we understand in life we are surrounded by and immersed in the "vital few" and "trivial many".

A few things are always more important than most things.

Regarding moving forward, producing results and getting where you ultimately want to go, most activity is a waste of time. A small minority of highly productive forces produce most good results. We waste a lot less time if we focus our efforts on those few highly productive forces; high performance habits.

Think about this: resources are always misallocated. You could say the forces of entropy are always at work. While our experience of life tends to demonstrate increasing complexity the natural state of systems is to tend toward equilibrium: for everything to settle and disperse equally. If we lack motivation, direction, and purpose we settle too; we misallocate our resources and our power.

Chapter 4: The Vital Few and Trivial Many

Life however, intends to grow and we are meant to create. Individually and collectively we contribute to life. Naturally we are meant to be increasing, renewing, growing. We are entrusted with this ability to add more to life, to bring more life into this world.

We are going to discuss this topic of adding more to life in detail in an upcoming chapter, for now, suffice it to say: we have to make things happen and if we apply ourselves at just the right time and place, with just the right effort, we can take advantage of leverage that produces exceptional results. High performance habits are the levers we need.

The *80/20 Rule* stipulates, and you know this from experience, a few people add most of the value. You want to be one of those few people. And if you want to experience an extraordinary level of success you want to associate with those few people in all areas of your life.

Take a second to think about how you use your time.

Typical people, people with long lists of things to do usually lament the fact that they don't have enough time.

Time is not the enemy. It's our use of time that is the problem.

There is no shortage of time. We get a new issue of 24 hours or 1,440 minutes or 86,400 seconds every single day. How are you using yours?

Chapter 4: The Vital Few and Trivial Many

If you want to accomplish something, if you want to get somewhere, you have to be using your time to move toward your objective; to enjoy a more full and fulfilling life.

Typically, mostly, usually our use of time is not rational.

Our most productive and most difficult use of time is thinking. Thinking is perhaps the most difficult of all human endeavors, but thinking is potentially also the most powerful. We find thinking so challenging though we avoid it like the plague. We usually keep ourselves so busy and distracted we barely devote any time at all to thinking. If you want to accomplish more, comply with the *80/20 Rule* and do less wasteful stuff. Instead think more.

If you want to double your productivity, cut the time you allocate to a task. Usually we consume most of the time we allocate to any given task with filler. Stop wasting time. That's what **High Performance Habits** is all about.

Use the unconventional wisdom of the *Pareto Principle* to focus your energy and stay on task. High performers use the *80/20 Rule* deliberately or instinctively to achieve phenomenal results. You can be a high performer too.

Become exceptionally productive. Take notice of those individuals and organizations that perform or produce well above the norm. They employ high performance habits. You can learn much by observing them closely.

Chapter 4: The Vital Few and Trivial Many

Look for the shortcut. Find the twenty percent solution. That is the solution where you select, develop, nurture and employ high performance habits.

The cumulative effect of employing the right habits over time will astound you.

Don't waste time being exhaustive. You can turn over every rock before you move forward. Be selective, make a wise, a considered choice, then advance. An imperfect solution executed vigorously will produce better results than a perfect solution never implemented.

Strive for excellence in a few things. No one is perfect. No one is exceptional at everything. Now, I'll give you, there are some exceptionally talented people out there. They are bright, good looking, and physically remarkable. These are rare specimens. It's too late to worry about what you didn't get naturally. Instead focus on the areas you show promise in. Focus on and develop your strengths. You can and will make extraordinary contributions if you stay focused and keep moving forward; if you develop the right habits.

Delegate and outsource the trivial things or the things you don't do well. We waste much too much time attempting to mitigate weaknesses when we should be reinforcing strengths. Other people can help take the burden off. Do what you enjoy the most and do what you do best.

Identify twenty percent habits; high performance habits; those activities that produce for you out-sized results. Focus your time, energy and talents on these. Work smarter, not

Chapter 4: The Vital Few and Trivial Many

harder. Work less but focus on targeted, limited, valuable goals.

As you proceed through *High Performance Habits* and begin developing high performance habits keep these 80/20 insights in mind:

Few people take objectives really seriously. One way to determine how much credence someone gives to a goal is to see if it is written down. If it's not in writing, it's probably just a wish. Wishes come and go quite easily.

Are your goals written down?

Achievers are selective and determined. Choose your allies carefully. You want to associate with people who are excited about achieving what you want to achieve. Success at anything is always a team effort. Choose the right competition, the right team and the right methods to achieve you goals.

Search for the few key inputs. These key inputs are usually not the obvious ones so search carefully.

A few events and decisions profoundly affect our lives. If you can anticipate these events, these moments, you can prepare for them and be ready to act to ensure the outcome you desire. Choosing and nurturing the right habits will prepare you for such defining moments.

You can achieve something significant with your life; the key is figuring out the right thing to do. Don't struggle figuring out the "long game," the "end-state," determine

Chapter 4: The Vital Few and Trivial Many

what you want the end-state to be then focus on developing habits that serve you. If you develop high performance habits you'll be moving in the right direction and the "end-state," the "long game," will come into focus. That vision you've created in your mind will begin to manifest in reality.

How far you go; how fast you go; even where you go are all determined by your core beliefs and the habits you build from those core beliefs. These habits are twenty percent causes; inputs that produce outsized results.

The point here is you have to focus, and you have to focus on the right things. Make the *80/20 Rule* work for you, not against you. Work the levers. Take control of your life.

Focusing on the right things; developing high performance habits; will allow you to make success a habit. With the right habits you'll achieve more and experience an extraordinary life.

Chapter 5
What Is a Habit?

Do you have any bad habits?

Do you bite your nails?

Are you constantly checking for texts, or tics; you can't put your smart phone down?

Do you snack late at night or watch a lot of TV?

How are your spending habits? Do you buy things impulsively?

Do you drink or smoke, or gamble compulsively?

Do you have a morning routine? Do you do the same things in the same way when you first get up? Say, head for the bathroom, shower, brush your teeth, then eat your breakfast or perhaps put on the coffee and read the paper; oh, I'm dating myself. Maybe you watch a morning show or check your favorite web feeds on your tablet or cell.

Do you do what you do every morning; execute your morning routine, with little conscious thought? If you changed just one item in your morning ritual would something feel wrong, just a little weird?

Do you consider your morning routine a habit?

Have you ever driven somewhere and been absorbed in thought or conversation so much that you couldn't

Chapter 5: What Is a Habit?

remember any of the details of the route you traveled? Have you been driving long enough that, for the most part, say when you are in light traffic and in familiar areas and not at all stressed about getting somewhere, driving is pretty routine? Driving then, for you has become habitual. You can drive mostly without consciously thinking. It's automatic.

Do you have habits of speech or thought?

Do you yourself, or maybe someone you know often say the same expressions repeatedly or possibly fill in dead space in conversations with noises like 'um' or 'uh' or with words and phrases like 'like' and 'you know'?

Some people use expletives as if they were conjunctions or adjectives. They fit into virtually every sentence and in nearly universal circumstances. Many people use filler noises or phrases or expletives and don't realize they do. These words and noises have become routine parts of their speech patterns. They have become habits.

If you were to measure out your entire day; consider your actions from waking in the morning to falling asleep at night, I bet you could come up with a number of habits; little routines you execute without consciously thinking; activities that don't require making deliberate, conscious choices. You would discover habits of feeling, habits of thinking and communicating, and habits of acting in most areas of your life: your personal, private life; with your relationships at work, with family and friends and out in the community.

Chapter 5: What Is a Habit?

Our lives are dominated by habits. Research suggests upwards of forty percent of our time is consumed by habits.

We human beings are a curious kind. We have drives and desires, wants and needs, motivations of all sorts. We have a universe of possibilities to pursue and a buffet of nearly unlimited selections from which to choose. Alas however, we are constrained. We have limited physical and intellectual capacity. We have the boundaries of time and distance to contend with, and we have all those competing drives and desires, wants and needs, demanding our time and attention.

A lot is happening. But we have an ingrained strategy to optimize results. We have our own means of executing the *80/20 Rule*.

We are hard-wired to balance options and effort for optimum result. We naturally seek out shortcuts. We want to get from "A" to "B" by the most direct and fastest route possible. The shortest distance between any two points is a straight line. If we can we'd rather skip the gap and move instantaneously from "A" to "B" without navigating that distance in between. We can hope anyway, can't we?

Now, I'm not trying to wipe the slate clean of various motivations and say we are slackers and schemers; though to a degree we all are. What I'm getting at is that we are by nature optimizers or maximizers. Given two choices, without any intervening motivational factors, we will always choose the one that gives the greatest reward for the least effort.

Chapter 5: What Is a Habit?

This tendency is consistent with the 80/20 principle we already discussed. The problem arises when we allow what happens naturally to get away from us.

Habits are a natural process of energy conservation. Habits help us get rewards for minimal effort. Unfortunately, quite often we develop habits that ultimately don't serve our long-term best interests.

Habits are our hard-wired means of optimizing the effort-reward conundrum we always face.

Life means action, effort. We must overcome a certain amount of resistance to just move, think of gravity, and we must overcome all kinds of obstacles to get anything or go anywhere.

Observing the happenings of life we can see that actions take place through a process, a cycle. Something initiates the cycle; a stimulus, a cue; we respond by feeling, we may or may not employ our faculty of mind, conscious thought, and we act to conclude, advance or resolve the process we empowered.

Since human life rests on and is ultimately driven by feelings, the simplified process we like to believe happens looks like this:

Feeling > Thought > Action > Result

In other words we encounter or manufacture a stimulus. Something cues us, or generates a feeling, a desire, a longing

Chapter 5: What Is a Habit?

within us. Being the rational, considerate beings we believe ourselves to be, we typically thoughtfully consider options and after careful, sensible deliberation we act.

Well, not really. If we are honest with ourselves, we know most often things don't happen this way. We do not think, we just act.

A simple, extreme example is what happens when your hand encounters a hot stove. You don't have the luxury of time for deliberation. 'Oh this is hot; it seems my skin may be burning.' No, you immediately react. Our bodies are a wonder that way. We have overriding built-in survival mechanisms to keep us safe. The reaction is automatic; no thinking required.

I'm not saying these biological reactions are habits, I'm just pointing out that we often act without thinking.

We move from stimulus, which ignites a feeling, immediately to action.

As I mentioned, some forty percent of what we do in life; forty percent of our time and activity; is consumed by habits, pre-determined routines of feeling, thinking, and mostly of acting.

Is that good or bad? Remember habits are a short cut; our means of maximizing reward while minimizing effort.

So just how do habits accomplish this magical result?

Habits eliminate thought from the process. With a habit the sequence looks like this:

Chapter 5: What Is a Habit?

Feeling > Action > Result > Thought

(The thought is usually a rationalization.)

Habits are our means of getting from "A" to "B" by the shortest route possible. Thinking is a time-consuming and for many a painfully difficult task, so why waste time and effort thinking? We are creatures of habit.

With the proper preparation; executing a routine sequence over and over again; we settle into a process that with minimal effort accomplishes our goal: optimum output. What we get is that feeling we are after. We navigate the path of least resistance by invoking or employing unconsciously a habit to ultimately achieve a satisfying feeling.

Habits can be a great thing. Habits can help; they help the super-successful perform at a high level; but the risk is quite frequently habits hurt. The wrong habits get in the way of us achieving our greatest desires; they get in the way of us becoming all we can be.

Lives can be dominated by bad habits: habits that don't serve our ultimate objectives. Bad habits meet temporary or convenient needs; they help us with the easy stuff. But they also undermine our progress. Bad habits get in our way. They hurt us. They harm us. They set us back.

If we want to travel far, soar high, perform at a high level, we must choose, develop and employ the right habits.

A complete habit cycle looks like this:

Chapter 5: What Is a Habit?

Cue > Craving > Routine > Reward

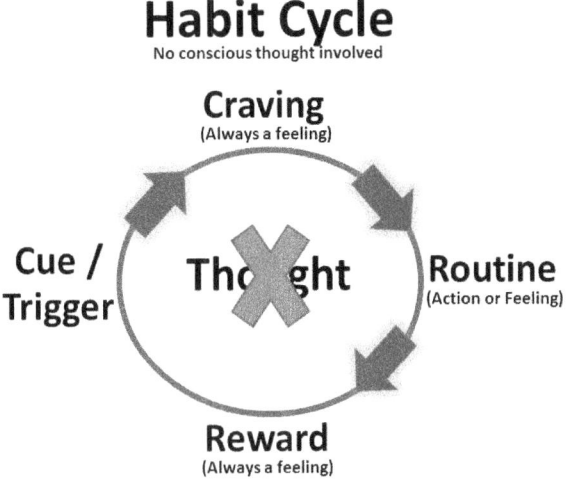

The fundamental components of our lives: feeling, thinking and acting fit into this habit cycle in the "Craving to Routine" part of the process. Life is fundamentally about feeling; that is we interpret experience and translate what we experience into feelings. How we feel about life, our success and our happiness depend on how we translate experience. Habits are shortcuts to get to feelings we enjoy or desire. For expediency we eliminate conscious thought – assessing, comparing, evaluating and choosing – from the habit cycle.

This habit cycle is a powerful natural process. Our purpose in *High Performance Habits* is to determine to put this process to good use. By adopting the right habits, high performance habits, we accelerate our progress and ensure our success.

Chapter 5: What Is a Habit?

Life naturally and automatically presents a stimulus or trigger; what comes next is up to us. Every ball is lobbed into our court. What we do with it, each ball, every ball, any ball, all balls, is our response to life. About forty percent of the time we respond by moving through a habit cycle. Are you moving the right way, the best way automatically?

Our daily lives are filled with cues and stimulus. Upon encountering a stimulus we can ignore it or empower it with desire, a craving arises. If we empower that stimulus, over time we enact a routine which proves to produce a reward; a means to fulfil that desire, satisfy that craving.

That stimulus acts as a trigger. We want that reward so we automatically execute the routine. If the routine works as it should, without any thought, we get the reward; that satisfying feeling. Life is good.

The question is: Are your habits serving or enslaving you?

Our beliefs about this world, ourselves and our place in it determine whether we opt for the path of least resistance as our life strategy. Our beliefs set our habits.

If we repeatedly encounter the same stimulus and energize the same desire we learn to employ a routine that gives us a satisfying reward. We quickly eliminate the need to think.

Chapter 5: What Is a Habit?

We go from cue to craving. The craving automatically initiates a routine. The routine in turn brings us the coveted reward. Aren't habits grand?

So here is your first activity in *High Performance Habits*. You are going to conduct a habit audit and produce a **Habits Inventory**.

You can do this by yourself, but it won't give you as comprehensive a result. You have to be very self-aware to be able to even recognize all the habits you currently employ. So if you have thick skin and some trusted allies solicit some assistance to help you with this inventory.

Over the course of a week, yes, seven full days, identify and catalog every habit you have.

Very quickly, within a few minutes you can come up with a list of known habits. These will range from simple things like stroking your hair, to drinking diet soda or coffee or other things, to watching late night television and constantly checking your smart phone.

List out every habit you know you have, but this is only the start of the inventory.

Over the course of the next week as you go through your days catalog every habit you employ. Write down those afternoon breaks. Write out your feelings and responses when you run into certain acquaintances or difficult coworkers. Write down every one of your habits.

Chapter 5: What Is a Habit?

This inventory is going to prove to be more challenging then you might first think. What I'm asking you to do is be in the moment, observant and thoughtful; all the time. This is not so easy.

If you have allies, at home and or at work, get them to audit your behavior over the course of this week. They don't have to say anything to you. Just ask them to write down every one of your habits they observe.

They will pick up speech patterns, little routines, even emotional responses you would not easily recognize.

At the end of the week, collect the lists from the people who agreed to help. Then compile one complete list of your current habits.

We are going to refer to and work with your **Habits Inventory** throughout this book; this *High Performance Habits* program. So make sure it's as complete as possible, legible and organized.

Habits drive our train.

Where is your train headed?

Are you on the fast track heading to where you want to go? Is everything falling in place in your life?

If your answers to these questions are yes, then keep doing what you are doing. Your habits are empowering you and moving you in the right direction.

Chapter 5: What Is a Habit?

If your answers to these questions are no, you've got some work to do.

You are currently employing low performance habits. What you must do is replace the low performance habits – the habits that are impeding your advance – with high performance habits. Then you'll be on the track to phenomenal achievement.

Conventional wisdom has long held that habits take about 21 days to coalesce. Actually habits can take as little as a day or as long as six months to develop. It's a matter of intensity of desire and the impact of the coveted reward.

If you have a wide array of habits to change don't worry so much about building habits in one day or one hundred. A journey of a thousand miles begins with a single step.

The most important thing is the next step; that's it. You are going to make progress one step at a time, one habit at a time.

This habit process is a tool. It's a tool we all use regularly. Your task now is to employ that tool, the habit process, for your ultimate benefit.

Take conscious control of your habit formation process. Make success a habit.

So where to start?

Chapter 5: What Is a Habit?

Well, first we're going to look into the life of someone who deliberately created habits for maximum impact. Then we are going to figure out just which habits are the right ones, the best ones for high performance.

Let's move into part two…

Part 2

High Performance Habits

HIGH PERFORMANCE HABITS

Chapter 6
Every Attempt a Learning Opportunity

Looking back over the last thousand years, from say the year 1,000 to the year 2,000, if we pick out the most influential figures, the men and women who shaped the course of history, we might choose Johannes Gutenberg who developed the printing press or Christopher Columbus or Galileo. Isaac Newton might be on our list or Martin Luther. These surely are men who shaped history. I want to introduce to you now someone who more than molded history. This individual influenced and continues to influence to this day virtually every aspect of your personal and professional life. This was the man who lit up the world and provided power to the masses.

Thomas Alva Edison is best known for his refinement of the electric light bulb and invention of the phonograph and the movie camera, but probably his most far reaching innovation was his process for generating and distributing electricity. Edison is the man who brought us light, where and when we need it.

The economical generation and distribution of electricity began the evolution of processes that regulate climate inside buildings, physically move people around the world and allow the mass of humanity to communicate instantaneously today. Edison's insights serve us like none other.

In his lifetime Edison secured some 1,093 patents in the United States alone. He held many more in Europe. He was a

Chapter 6: Every Attempt a Learning Opportunity

prolific inventor, a perceptive scientist and an accomplished business man. But, you might not have bet on his success had you known him as a child and young man.

Fortunately for all the people who have benefitted and will yet benefit from his genius Thomas Edison forged high performance habits from the beginning. These habits served him, and us, well.

Thomas was the youngest of seven children. As an infant he suffered a bout with scarlet fever that severely limited his ability to hear. Through his life, though he recognized this disability, he never let his hearing loss slow him down. He believed his deficiency hearing provided him a greater ability to think.

Thomas didn't learn to speak until he was four years old. Once he could communicate though he began to take the world by storm.

The epitome of an inquisitive youngster, Thomas peppered his parents with questions about everything. He wanted to know how things work and why. With a house full of children and other competing interests to attend to Thomas' parents channeled his energy and his voracious appetite for learning as best they could.

At the age of seven Thomas attempted to begin a formal classroom education. His teacher, trying to manage a single-room schoolhouse with 38 children determined Thomas was hyperactive and prone to distraction. Thomas' teacher labeled him "difficult." We might label him ADHD (attention deficit hyperactivity disorder) today. Of course our solution for ADHD is drugs. Back then support was the order of the day. When

Chapter 6: Every Attempt a Learning Opportunity

Thomas' mother Nancy Edison, a gifted teacher in her own right, realized school was not going well for Thomas she settled on a better route, home schooling, and got to work.

Edison's mother was the defining influence of his life. She nurtured him, encouraged him and directed him. She believed in him so much he couldn't help but believe in himself. Nancy focused Thomas' education on mastering reading, writing, and arithmetic with a solid grounding in the *Bible*. Thomas' father for his part encouraged the young student to read the classics.

Thomas was so enthralled by learning that when first introduced to a library he committed to start in one corner and systematically read every book on every shelf. His parents convinced him there was a better approach to learning and a more efficient use of his time and energy.

Thomas Edison had ambition and desire, but also recognized he possessed limitations. He developed a unique process of independent learning and self-education that carried him through a lifetime of scientific and industrial exploration and achievement.

Early on as he labored through the classics, like Newton's *Principia*, Edison was disillusioned by obscure, aristocratic language. He was enthralled however, by the pure genius of the concepts, the theories and the laws most clearly defined through mathematics. Edison recognized at an early age what wisdom he could glean from the lives and writings of great men and women, but he also internalized the fact that these writers could be caught in traps of self-deception and error. So he tested every relevant theory he came across to prove the concept for

Chapter 6: Every Attempt a Learning Opportunity

himself. His thoroughness and attention to detail helped him avoid those traps of self-deception as best he could.

Along with his habit of personal growth and development, and really as a means to further it, Edison cultivated nearly unwavering perseverance. He kept at a task, no matter how challenging until he had it figured out. This single trait put him in a class by himself. He was not to be one who stopped short of the finish line. What others termed as failures Edison saw as learning attempts. He didn't fail; he discovered ways things wouldn't work.

At the age of twelve Edison decided it was time; time to make his own way. He started selling newspapers and snacks on the local train. He built a business where he managed other boys doing the selling and he even started publishing and distributing his own newspaper. His publishing business was so profitable he was able to furnish an extensive laboratory to facilitate his experimentation. Everything didn't always go smoothly however. A makeshift lab Edison built on a rail baggage car set fire to the train. He lost access to the railroad.

A fortuitous event helped Edison secure a position as a telegraph operator. He positioned himself at the cutting edge of technology and became somewhat of a journeyman operator, traveling around the Midwest for five years pursuing opportunity while continuing to tinker. Upon stopping back to check in on his family he saw his parents were not doing well. He decided he had to buckle down and make things happen. On the advice of a friend, he took a permanent telegraph operator position with Western Union in Boston, Massachusetts, a hub for learning and the development of cutting edge technology.

Chapter 6: Every Attempt a Learning Opportunity

While working 12-hour days, six days a week for Western Union Edison continued to experiment and tinker. His first patent was for an automated vote counting machine. After much effort he realized no one wanted his device. Motivated by this disheartening experience he resolved to focus on inventing things that could succeed in the marketplace; devices people would want to buy.

Edison's employers at Western Union were growing impatient with his moonlighting ventures which were distracting from his job performance. So Edison borrowed money from a friend and headed for the "Big Apple." After a few weeks in New York Edison was struggling not so much to succeed, but to survive. Then another fortuitous event reestablished him on his path.

After begging for money in the financial district Edison began wandering through buildings. He came across a financial services manager all in a tizzy. His stock ticker had stopped working and no one could figure it out. Having been sleeping in the basements of office buildings in the financial district Edison had already acquainted himself with these devices. He gave it a go and easily corrected the breakage. He was hired on the spot for a salary of $300 per month.

Seeing a need Edison went on to develop improvements to stock ticker technology and at the age of twenty-two sold the rights to these improvements for $40,000; a substantial sum at the time.

With this seed money Edison set up a small laboratory and manufacturing facility in Newark, New Jersey. He grew that

Chapter 6: Every Attempt a Learning Opportunity

laboratory into the first mass-production research facility in the world. Edison hired and allied himself with other creative ambitious men and went on to unparalleled achievements inventing, developing businesses and industrial processes, and advancing the industrial revolution.

Thomas Edison was a man with a big appetite for learning. From humble beginnings he built an industrial empire. He recognized his own shortcomings early on. Instead of letting his weaknesses slow him down he focused on his strengths and built on success. He vowed to not worry about things beyond his control. Perseverance and a willingness to go where others had not ventured set him apart from the masses. No attempt was wasted. Every attempt was a learning opportunity.

Thomas Edison adopted habits which always kept him moving forward. He became affectionately known as the Wizard of Menlo Park; an extraordinary success.

His high performance habits lit up our lives.

Chapter 7
The Right Habits

Thomas Edison and Andrew Carnegie exhibited remarkably similar characteristics. They both used high performance habits to achieve phenomenal success. They both worked diligently on improving themselves; they were always learning. They had the habit of always going the extra mile; doing more than was required. They had the habit of being open to opportunity; they were willing to move forward and take measured risks. And they had the habit of networking; of building partnerships and deliberately associating with and surrounding themselves with exceptional people. These were the habits that made the "Prince of Steel" and the "Wizard of Menlo Park".

Super successful people either instinctively or consciously and deliberately choose, develop and nurture habits that allow them to move faster, travel farther and accomplish more than the average masses of the great unwashed. High achievers leverage the RIGHT HABITS; habits that make all the difference.

What about you?

Do any of these routines lay claim to your time, energy and talents?

Watching television excessively (enough to interrupt other activities including sleep).

Nail biting or playing with your hair.

Chapter 7: The Right Habits

Constantly checking your smartphone or posting useless information to the net.

Snacking compulsively or eating too much processed or fast food.

Over spending or impulsively shopping.

Smoking or drinking.

Routinely interrupting other people when they speak.

Avoiding eye contact.

Peppering your speech with "um", "ah", "like", "you know" or expletives.

We're all familiar with bad habits. We recognize them in other people right away, but we rarely recognize them in ourselves. This list of "bad" habits is a selection of some of the most common habits people settle into.

Each habit routine is a process that begins with a cue stirring up a craving and ends with some level of satisfaction – a feeling reward. We employ habits to meet our needs; even needs that ultimately limit us, hold us back, and keep us from achieving our potential.

Many of the needs we satisfy by means of habit, particularly bad habits, those habits that don't serve us, are unconscious. We are not even aware we have these habits. Our core beliefs about the world, ourselves and our place in it have nurtured these habits.

We often opt for the comfort of the known over the discomfort of the unknown. We choose the cropped effort of

Chapter 7: The Right Habits

a routine over the pain and discomfort required to exert ourselves to surge down a new path.

The bad habits I mentioned earlier are examples of observable habit cycles. They include observable physical routines.

More insidious and potentially more limiting are our habits of mind, or thought habits. These are thinking loops that can significantly impact our lives and inhibit the expression of our vast potential.

We establish thought patterns to achieve the same ends as action habits. We unconsciously want to feel good or at least feel better about ourselves and we don't want to expend too much effort. Instead of exerting ourselves examining a new perspective we just adopt a mental shortcut; a habit of thought.

Habits of thought can stilt our thinking and draw in the boundaries of our minds. We in effect think ourselves into a box, all to make life easier. What we end up doing is make life worse.

So, if we want to change; if we want to become super-successful, high-achievers and perform at a consistently high level we have to choose, develop and nurture high performance habits. By thinking and acting the right way, the best way possible, we will, in the long run go farther, do more and feel better.

High performance habits allow us to realize our potential and achieve our ultimate purpose. As a high performer you

Chapter 7: The Right Habits

will do more, have more, and be more. Choose the right habits.

Just what are the right habits? What are the habits high performers employ?

High performers are positive, confident, grateful people, open to opportunity and willing to take calculated risks.

High performers take care of themselves. They are active. Many exercise regularly; they are healthy and fit. They rest and recuperate; deliberately scheduling down time.

High performers have a growth mindset. They embrace the challenge and revel in the adventure of life. They develop themselves. They are lifelong learners.

High performers take time regularly to think, reflect, meditate, pray. They nurture a thankful attitude and cultivate a worthwhile and motivating vision.

High performers focus their efforts intensely. They eliminate distractions and see projects through. They create rather than compete. This is an area we will explore in more detail later, but for now realize truly high performers work to fulfill their potential, not get ahead by knocking other people down.

And high performers persist; they keep going, despite the odds, despite the pain. They routinely do what average people refuse to do.

Chapter 7: The Right Habits

High performers constantly seek to improve their communication and interpersonal skills but they are selective with social interaction. They ally with, and surround themselves with positive, capable, uplifting people. They build and maintain support networks of like-minded, success-oriented individuals.

High performers, in effect, do not distinguish between "work" and "life". They do what they love to do. To them work is play. Whatever they are doing is celebrated as part of the adventure.

This does sound like a pretty tall order – that is being a high performer. Remember though, this disposition, this attitude, these habits are an outcome of core beliefs – beliefs high performers have about the world, themselves and their place in it. They are connected; they are confident; and they see no way to go but forward.

You can be this way too. You can realize so much more. You have potential you have not begun to tap.

Do you have the desire to change?

Do you have the desire to soar?

High performers use the same 24 hours a day everyone else has and the same thought energy everyone else has access to, but they use these differently. Because of their core beliefs and the discipline of cultivating productive habits, they intentionally and deliberately optimize their use of time and energy.

Chapter 7: The Right Habits

High performers develop the right habits for phenomenal success.

Now, it's not that every high performer has adopted each of these habits. Some high achievers live "in balance" over the long term. Others surge to new heights, then rest and recuperate after moving forward. Some struggle their entire lives in some areas even while they are super-successful in others.

No one is perfect and no life is a straight shot to the top. High performers struggle and fail, stumble and fall, but they always get up, they always try again. High performers find meaning and joy in the effort. We can learn to do that too.

High achievers don't necessarily eliminate bad habits from their repertoire of activities. It's just that, in balance, they synergize their efforts with others and move forward. They grow like life intends to grow. High performers create and achieve in concert with life. In balance, their habits serve them and move them in the right direction.

You should recognize from this list; the habits high performers embody – these are tasks, habits, you can develop and you can employ. If you do things a certain way, if you do things that high achievers do, you can't help but be successful. The challenge of course is making the switch; working through the change; going through, around or over the obstacles and overcoming the resistance that holds you back.

Chapter 7: The Right Habits

You have to change yourself to change your circumstances and that change starts right here – with choosing the right habits.

You can put in the hours and work hard. You can contribute untold effort, but if you are not heading in the right direction – developing and cultivating the right habits – you are not going to realize your true potential.

Can you see that now?

Choose and cultivate the right habits.

Look back at the **High Performance Habits Summary** – that list you just reviewed or the one reproduced in Appendix A – and pull out your **Habits Inventory**; that list of your habits you constructed. Examine and compare both lists.

What you need to know is not all habits are created equal. The *80/20 Rule* applies to habits. Some habits matter more than others.

The habits that most directly spring from your core beliefs about the world, yourself, and your place in it are the habits that matter most.

Those far-reaching, high impact habits are known as "keystone" habits; or what I like to call "lever" habits. A keystone is a foundational or pivotal component of a structure. These key or lever habits generate disproportional effect; they are levers directly impacting your core beliefs.

Chapter 7: The Right Habits

If your lever habits are right they will naturally cause you to make changes to other habits. Changing these lever habits creates a far-reaching ripple effect.

Here are two examples.

First, exercise is a keystone or lever habit. If you adopt exercise as a daily habit, your body will respond and your mindset will begin to change. If you make exercise a habit, something you do automatically every day, routinely, you will begin to think of yourself as someone who is active and over time fit. With that change in mindset you will become more aware of your eating habits. Thinking of yourself as someone who is fit and healthy will influence your food choices. Thinking of yourself as someone who cares about your body and physical performance will influence your television watching habits and likely impact your sleep routine. These changes in turn will impact your attitude. Exercise is a lever habit.

The second example of a lever habit is adopting a growth mindset. We know life is changing; life is dynamic. The most intelligent and wisest men and women in history realized that the more they learned, the less they knew. Life is an ever unfolding adventure. Too often we settle into a mindset that says we know it all, or at least we believe we know enough. We determine that we've arrived.

Continuing to learn, to try new things, to develop and grow means we aren't all that. We don't know everything. We aren't the top of the heap, the greatest. The opposite of a growth mindset, as Carol Dweck explains in her bestselling

Chapter 7: The Right Habits

book *Mindset, The New Psychology of Success*, is a fixed mindset. Having a fixed mindset is all about validating our value. A fixed mindset never serves us. Changing our thinking – changing our approach to life – becoming a life-long learner on a journey of exploration and growth will fundamentally alter our habits of mind and action. Adopting a growth mindset changes core beliefs and widely influences our habits. Our mindset, the state, attitude or disposition of our mind, is a lever habit.

Adopting and developing a keystone or lever habit will cause broad changes across various areas of your life. Developing a lever habit that works in a positive way will ultimately influence your core beliefs. Once your beliefs change your life will profoundly change.

Again, compare those two lists: your **Habits Inventory** and the **High Performance Habits Summary**. Look at your inventory of habits. Break the list into two parts. Make a list of the habits you believe that serve you and a list of the habits you believe that hurt you.

Are any of the habits that serve you now similar to those listed on the **High Performance Habits Summary**?

What you are starting to do here, by answering these questions and making this comparison, is to determine which habits you might want to eliminate.

Begin to think about which high performance habits you might like to adopt as well.

Chapter 7: The Right Habits

We'll explore these high performance habits in more detail in the next chapters in this section and in **Part 3**. It's in **Part 4** where the real work begins.

Let's keep moving forward. In the next chapter we focus more closely on specific high performance habits.

Chapter 8
Attitude and Mindset

For some life is brief in time; for others life is brief in exploit. For daring souls however, life is a magnificent adventure; an opportunity to achieve and experience, an opportunity to connect and create, and an opportunity to be and become. The essence of the human experience is a collective expression of growth; relating and creating.

The instruction manual for life might be summed up in this one statement:

Relate to what you encounter and create what the world lacks.

Our purpose is not to take from this world, to get – our purpose, our reason for being – is to give. We each, you and I, are conduits for the energy of life. Creating is our contribution to life; relating to creation is our reward.

We each bring to the world the ability to express potential, to create, to add to life. It's an exciting opportunity.

The Cherokee Indians anticipate the expression of potential this way:

When you were born, you cried and the world rejoiced. Live your life so that when you die, the world cries and you rejoice.

Chapter 8: Attitude and Mindset

If you succeed in this, you will have used your time, energy and talents well.

So let's get busy. Opportunities are unlimited but our time is not.

We are taking a closer look at what I call lever habits; those habits that leverage the energy of life to allow us to perform at our best – to become high performers.

Let's delve into the most powerful lever of them all: our mindset.

Think for a minute about Carnegie and Edison. Do you remember what set these two remarkable individuals apart from the masses? The habits they developed and nurtured. The habit of personal development; the habit of always going the extra mile and doing more than was required; the habit of being open to opportunity, willing to take risks to advance; and of course the habit of building a network of extraordinary people. Carnegie and Edison both had positive attitudes and growth-oriented mindsets.

You've heard about the power of positive thinking. You are familiar with, and perhaps have even come to believe that having a positive attitude toward the task at hand, the circumstances and people you encounter, and toward life in general, offers a distinct advantage.

A positive attitude combined with a growth mindset separates the doers and achievers from all the rest. High

Chapter 8: Attitude and Mindset

performers nurture and deliberately cultivate the habit of employing a positive attitude and a growth mindset.

High performers operate on the human default setting; the setting for maximum performance.

The approach high performers take to life is one of opportunity and possibility. They are always learning, always growing, always advancing, always creating.

For them, for high performers, failure is not an option, not because they can do everything well and they succeed at everything they try, but because every attempt is a learning experience, an opportunity to grow.

High performers only accept good enough if it moves them on to something even greater. They are not content to just get by. High performers want to test their limits. High performers want to express their full potential. Once they set their sights on a goal, once they choose a course and determine a direction they always go the extra mile. If they can do better, if they have the time and energy to produce a better result, they will. Average is not satisfactory – exceptional is a high performer's standard.

A positive attitude, growth mindset is a state of being creative, not competitive. The *Source* is a well-spring of unlimited supply. Positive attitude, growth mindset people – high performers – recognize this truth.

The world is not a place of lack; it's a place of abundance. High performers don't have to put anyone down

Chapter 8: Attitude and Mindset

so they can climb up. They don't have to beat someone out to get what they want. They don't out-play, out-wit, out-last to survive. People with a positive attitude and growth mindset, people who nurture a state of mind that sees the world as a playground and obstacles as challenges to help them grow, are unstoppable. They are properly grounded; connected to the *Source*.

Before I raise the bar too high and suggest that high performers are superhuman, I should point out, no one, no one maintains a high energy, positive connection all the time. It's a matter of tipping the balance in our favor.

High performers maintain a positive attitude, growth mindset most of the time. Because they do, they are willing to advance, energized to advance, and motivated to advance. High performers recognize immediately when they encounter or settle into a negative or fixed mindset. They jump into action to get out of the negative state as quickly as possible.

Sustaining a positive attitude and growth mindset in itself takes disciplined effort. It requires taking care of our bodies; maintaining our health and fitness, getting enough rest and taking the time to recharge. It requires feeding our minds with positive inspiration regularly and associating with positive, like-minded people as often as possible; the more often the better. It requires focusing on worthwhile, creative tasks and setting goals that are challenging and achievable. And it requires building and sustaining a network of support; people to call on and collaborate with and rely on. High performers know no one succeeds alone.

Chapter 8: Attitude and Mindset

Thought is the most powerful tool we have in our kit bag, our toolbox for life. Thought is the means we use to bridge the gap between the reality of circumstance, the world out there, and the potential, the supply of the unlimited *Source*. Building and maintaining an attitude and mindset that is in-synch with the *Source* means our core beliefs are that all is right with the world, we are safe and connected, competent and capable, and we have purpose, a reason for being.

Cultivating the habit of a positive attitude and growth mindset is the preeminent lever to change your life – it is the quintessential high performance habit.

People with positive attitudes are optimistic, confident, grateful people. They nurture a thankful disposition and cultivate a worthwhile and motivating vision. They've got things to do, places to go, and people to see. The opportunity is now, why waste time? They realize life is not a sure thing and sometimes they have to advance blindly. They are willing to take risks. They embrace the challenge and relish the adventure of life.

High performers have a growth mindset. They are lifelong learners. They maintain their bodies and cultivate their minds. They take time daily to connect with the *Source*.

Given they are immersed in the adventure, high performers attempt not to waste time. They focus their efforts intensely. They are goal oriented. And to accomplish

Chapter 8: Attitude and Mindset

their goals as quickly and as competently as possible they maintain a single-minded focus.

To ensure this single-mined focus they eliminate distractions. Having set worthwhile goals they persist. At times they find maybe the method or process they employ is not correct. Maybe the route they choose is not the best one, so they change course. They just don't give up. Vision and persistence are hallmarks of high performers; they are staples of the positive mindset.

High performers go the extra mile and do what needs to be done. They do what average performers refuse to do.

A positive attitude and growth mindset is a force to use across all dimensions of life: physical, mental, emotional, spiritual, social, and material. A positive attitude and growth mindset allow opportunity and creativity to flow.

That attitude and mindset are grounded in those core beliefs we talked about. A positive attitude and growth mindset are the manifestation of positive core beliefs. This means, if you aren't positive most of the time now and if you don't routinely intend to grow, you might not want to tackle this biggest lever habit of them all first.

Not that you can't change your attitude and mindset habits, you can. The challenge is, you've got an awful lot of baggage you are carrying around.

A starting point may be to change your attitude and your mindset, by situation; in an individual habit cycle. Over

Chapter 8: Attitude and Mindset

time, taking on one habit after another you can tip the balance. Your habits will change, your attitude and mindset will change, your core beliefs will change and your performance will skyrocket.

We'll get into the details of how in **Part 4**, but now before we wrap up this session I want to set the stage for where we are headed next.

We have just reviewed the most powerful habit levers of them all – attitude and mindset. In the next chapter we focus on making an impression and improving self-confidence.

Habits of conduct and health may be the most practical place to begin to change personal habits; to being your habits change process.

Strengthening your body and building your confidence may be the best place to start the habit reformation process.

Succeeding is really all about developing the right habits. By choosing and developing the right habits you make success a habit.

HIGH PERFORMANCE HABITS

Chapter 9
Make an Impression

We've talked about the right habits; those keystone or lever habits to focus on. The lives of Carnegie and Edison and other great men and women, demonstrate high performers' exhibit – embody – a certain way of doing things. Truly great men and women, men and women who achieve exceptional results over time, make success a habit. They adopt, develop and nurture specific habits of thought, habits of feeling and habits of action.

High performers operate from a foundation of core beliefs that recognize the world as an inviting place where opportunity abounds. High performers believe they themselves are capable and worthy. And high performers believe that they have a place in and a purpose for being in this world. They spend their time, energy and talents immersed in the adventure; moving forward and making things happen.

Success in life hinges on our core beliefs. But, as we've discussed, core beliefs are built over time and reside deep and protected in our unconscious minds. We make the world conform to the reality we define with our core beliefs.

If we are wallowing in mediocrity our core beliefs are not serving us. To change course, to improve the conditions outside we have to change our core beliefs inside.

Change is always an inside job.

Chapter 9: Make an Impression

Our rational conscious mind tells us that we see the world as it is and we deal with it as best we can. We react to circumstances, often automatically. We resist the idea that we ourselves may in fact be creating the world we think is out there.

This world we create is an interpretation of what is, made to conform to the programming of core beliefs. So let's start chiseling away at those core beliefs that are not serving us. Let's start changing our core from the outside in.

Our most important lever habit is our dominant state of mind.

Thought is a powerful tool; the most powerful tool we human beings have access to. High performers maintain a positive, open, non-judgmental, growth-oriented state of mind. They approach life as a series of adventures with challenges to overcome. They maintain an unwavering faith in their ability to move forward and succeed. They do not allow fear, or resistance to change, to hold them back from realizing the results and manifesting the reality they desire.

Do you have a positive attitude and growth-oriented mindset most of the time?

If not, let's start doing something about that right now.

Where we are ultimately headed is to ignite a spark deep in our subconscious that will glow and grow into a self-sustaining positive mindset. But we have to break through

Chapter 9: Make an Impression

the protective barriers we built to stabilize and ensure our core beliefs.

You've heard it said, 'You don't get a second chance to make a first impression.' Well that may be true specifically, that is a first impression is the only first impression, but you do have repeated opportunities to make an impression.

In this chapter we focus on making an impression. Specifically we explore and work with this idea of making an impression two ways:

First, we never work alone; we don't succeed alone. We are always making impressions on other people. The surest and shortest route to success is by collaborating with other people, so it's important that we make a good impression on others.

Second, we want to impress ourselves. What we put out, what we give off into the world is reflected back to us. Other people observe, absorb and interpret our energy then reflect our energy back to us. If the impression we consistently, habitually make is positive we are going to get back a positive reflection from the world. If we are open to these impressions even the slightest bit, they will influence our core beliefs.

All that sounds very theoretical, and if I haven't lost you completely you're probably wondering: 'When are we going to get practical?' Right now.

Chapter 9: Make an Impression

The ultimate state of high performers, that is, how they come across to others, is confident. They may not have all the answers, they may not be masters of every skill but they are comfortable in their own skin and confident in their abilities to deal with whatever circumstances they find themselves in. They know they can grow and they are willing to try. The confidence high performers' exhibit springs from core beliefs.

If you don't have the core belief that exhibits confidence, don't worry. We can change that.

And, by the way, don't get me wrong, I'm not talking about an attitude that attempts to dominate or demean others. That is not true confidence. A demeaning or arrogant attitude is fear, insecurity and ignorance showing through. What I mean by confidence is someone who meets the world on their own terms, not someone who is insecure and attempting to get others or the world to validate them as worthy. What I'm talking about is genuine confidence. You know what I mean.

To build that confidence we need to adopt some basic habits.

Before you consider these simple habits to make an impression, I want to caution you. You may think these suggestions are shallow and this is not where real confidence springs from. That may be true – true confidence radiates from the inside out – but there are only two ways to change core beliefs and they are interrelated.

Chapter 9: Make an Impression

The power of an individual's will, that connection to the *Source* I introduced early on can motivate someone to overcome circumstances and instill core beliefs that manifest a calm and confident demeanor.

The other way to influence core beliefs is through that network of people that we interact with. If the people around us reinforce positive traits and attributes – if they demonstrate the world is a safe place and that we are capable and valued and have a place and purpose – we are likely to build and maintain corresponding core beliefs.

Change is an inside job, powered from the inspiration of the *Source* and powered by the inspiration of others. The inspiration of other people is an expression of the *Source* in the world around us.

I hope I'm not confusing you.

My point is: goodness, love, and truth all originate from the same source. That *Source*, that power, can reach us from the inside. It's the spark that allows people to overcome immense obstacles when seemingly all circumstances are stacked against them. Or that power can reach us as expressions through the people and the environment that surround us. It's always raining blessings. If we open ourselves to the goodness, love and truth that shower us we will naturally reorder our core beliefs and life will change.

At this point in the program we are deliberately going after that external energy. By changing what we express, making our expressions of life more positive, we will receive back more positive reflections. We will change the world

Chapter 9: Make an Impression

out there by changing ourselves in here. We will express more positive growth energy, which will in turn be reflected back to us. We then can absorb what we need to continue to change.

How we act, how we move our bodies, how people react to us are all reflections of ourselves. We can influence what's inside by changing our image outside.

We have to start somewhere.

So let's work on our appearance.

Here is a simple list, organized by actions that require the least effort to enact to the most effort to enact. Remember now, making these actions serve you only really requires effort until the action becomes a habit. Once you've made these actions routine they will be effortless.

1. Smile.

2. Present a Confident Posture.

3. Always be Well Groomed.

4. Dress Up (Be Well Clothed).

5. Get Fit.

Are these some of your habits? Do you routinely smile and make eye contact? Do you stand up straight, with your weight balanced and your shoulders back and relaxed? Do you pay attention to hair and makeup, nails and cleanliness? Do you dress appropriately; in other words do you take some care to wear clean, pressed clothing, properly matched and

Chapter 9: Make an Impression

appropriate for the occasion? Do you maintain a healthy weight and a strong fit body?

Each of these impression-making activities can be made into a habit.

Our ultimate goal here is to improve our confidence. If you diligently and methodically begin to remake yourself in these five areas you will begin to generate positive, supportive feedback from other people.

You may not initially see yourself as self-confident, as someone who has it together, but if you continue to work on these expressions of yourself you soon will. And once you see yourself as self-confident you will be.

A smile is a natural way to demonstrate joy and acceptance. Developing a natural, friendly smile and offering it routinely shows people you are welcoming and unafraid. Start smiling more today. It's an easy thing to do. And even if you don't feel like smiling at first, override those feelings and start smiling more. Practice in the mirror if you have to. If you practice and stick with it, you'll notice when you smile you will feel different. Up till now smiling has been in response to a feeling. What I'm asking you to do is smile no matter how you feel and you'll find that the act of smiling will make you feel better. Give it a try.

Our posture, good, bad or indifferent, is another expression of a feeling. From an observers perspective bad posture demonstrates a lack of confidence, a lack of focus,

Chapter 9: Make an Impression

and a lack of passion. Standing stooped with shoulders rolled forward, arms tense and eyes down demonstrates a weak and unsure demeanor. Like with a smile, our posture is normally the result of a feeling – usually a habitual feeling.

So let's now deliberately use our posture to change how we feel. Standing in a confident posture: body erect, chest forward, shoulders back, arms relaxed and eyes alert, actually makes us feel more confident and capable. We look more confident and capable to other people as well. Try it.

You can change how you feel by what you do. Yes you can.

We have developed certain postures over time. Changing your posture, your body position, how you direct your eyes, even the expression on your face is going to take concerted effort. You won't be able to remake these habits in a day. And I'm not asking you to start right this minute. We are going to approach this habit change process very deliberately in **Part 4**, but for now I want you to recognize the big impact small changes can make.

If you are not confident now, then smile and posture may be where you begin your habits change process. But let's continue looking at some other habits that make an impression.

A couple of relatively easy habits to change, though again they will take effort, are your habits of personal grooming and how you dress. Some people resist this idea,

Chapter 9: Make an Impression

the notion that how we look matters. How we present ourselves to the world is a reflection of what we believe about ourselves. Looking sloppy and unkempt communicates to others and expresses much about ourselves.

If you are one of those that doubts that how you look matters, then I will ask you to just conduct an experiment. Make a change.

For a week, a full week, neaten and clean yourself up. Dress up and present yourself to the world in a new way. Interact with people in places that are out of your norm. If you are used to hanging out in sweats with friends making a change and hanging out more neatly dressed is not going to give you genuine feedback. Go to places and interact with people you aspire to associate with. See what kind of feedback you get. If it's positive you're on the right track.

And finally I've used the word fit on my list of habits. Two thirds of American adults are overweight or obese. Far too many people are settling. These people are passing on realizing their full potential.

Exercise is a lever habit. If you want to change yourself in a big way get more active. You can start small and build, but if you really want to change your life, if you want to do more, have more and become more, make yourself healthy and fit.

Exercise may be the best habit to begin with when you undertake the habit change process.

Chapter 9: Make an Impression

In **Part 1**, we covered the big picture. Life is built on a foundation of core beliefs; beliefs about the world, ourselves and our place in this world.

Some things matter more than others. For our purposes, some habits have greater impact and allow more leverage than others.

In this section we focused on choosing the right habits: high performance habits.

In the next section, **Part 3**, we focus on social habits; habits of communicating and relating, and habits of building teams and leading.

Life is a team sport. It's all about relationships. Getting relationships right is an essential component of high achievement.

High performers are connected. They are connected with the *Source* and they are connected with other people.

Connected we can do anything.

Together, in cooperation with, and in collaboration with, other similarly motivated individuals we can quickly adopt new habits. We can transform ourselves into the high performers we are meant to be.

Part 3

You are NOT Alone

HIGH PERFORMANCE HABITS

Chapter 10
Relationships Make or Break

How does a desperately poor, extremely disadvantaged, abused young girl overcome nearly insurmountable obstacles and the worst of circumstances to become one of the wealthiest and most influential people in the world?

We tend to think we have few advantages and that we face difficult challenges. Well, see how your experience measures up.

This woman was born to a poor, unmarried teenage mother in rural Mississippi. Her mother survived on welfare and paltry earnings working as a maid.

Our young heroin was raised in abject poverty. At times the only clothes she had were fashioned from potato sacks. Unable to find work locally her mother headed north to Milwaukee in search of opportunity. For the first six years of her life she lived with her mother's mother; the most influential figure in her childhood. Her grandmother planted the seeds of learning and nurtured the promise of better things to come.

After a time this young girl traveled north to reunite with her mother. Beginning at the age of nine, she was repeatedly sexually abused by male relatives and friends of her mother. Life was harsh, to say the least.

Chapter 10: Relationships Make or Break

By the age of thirteen, nearly hopeless, she ran away from home only to soon find herself pregnant and alone. Her child, a baby boy, died shortly after birth.

Doesn't this sound like a tale of desperation and tragedy? You imagine this story ending on a cold slab in a morgue or in the steely, cramped confines of a prison cell. How does one change course when all the momentum of life is pushing you down a path of desolation, of desperation? How do you keep hope alive? How can there be hope when there seems to be no light?

Despite her dire circumstances Oprah Winfrey always had hope. She was bright, she was beautiful, she had unique gifts and talents and, at the most fortuitous of times, at precisely the right junctures in her life, she got the support she needed to keep moving forward. Somehow the right people were always there when she needed them.

People who knew Oprah, people who had vision beyond the slums, believed in her.

With seemingly all the odds stacked against her, Oprah did the best she could with what she had and kept moving forward. She continued to ask, she continued to search, and she continued to knock. Doors opened. Those openings, those passages leading forward, were by means of new people and new relationships.

Oprah Winfrey is the personification of perseverance; of someone who kept moving forward, who listened to the still quiet voice, who took chances and believed in something better despite appearances and despite the conditions that

Chapter 10: Relationships Make or Break

surrounded her. She had reason to fear. She had reason to be suspicious of other people, but her trust, her faith in herself and other people was stronger. She took chances. She trusted trustworthy people and they helped her succeed.

People recognize and connect to the hope Oprah Winfrey exemplifies. Oprah is not perfect, she has her challenges. She struggles still, but she presses on. That's why so many people identify with her. That's why so many people trust her.

Oprah's fans and admirers realize that Oprah's light of hope burns for more than Oprah herself. Oprah's light of hope burns for everyone who faces obstacles, everyone who struggles with demons, everyone who intends to move forward.

Oprah connects with people. She is genuine. She is real. And she cares. These are traits that are in short supply in the public sphere.

Over the course of about a decade Oprah went from public school student to queen of daytime television. Her meteoric rise was nothing short of astonishing. How was this possible?

Oprah's mother was struggling in Milwaukee trying to make ends meet and provide for more children when Oprah rebelled – as we now know, for good reason. She was sent to Nashville to live with the person she believed to be her biological father.

Chapter 10: Relationships Make or Break

Her father established some boundaries. He was strict but encouraged learning. Oprah settled into an environment where for the first time in her life she felt she fit in. She took on the yoke of self-discipline and made a decision to change course. She replaced some old discouraging habits with new promising ones. She began to focus on her studies; soon becoming an honors student. She changed her attitude; made it positive, and she changed her mindset; she decided to grow through her difficulties.

For the first time in her life she saw opportunities and remembering her grandmother's guidance, she pursued them. People were there for her, their arms outstretched. She only needed to grab hold. The light of hope that she nurtured as a flicker began to glow steady and then began to burn brighter.

She mustered up the courage to step out of her comfort zone and take risks. Her grandmother had encouraged her to leverage her strengths; she did.

Oprah joined the school's speech team. She placed second nationally in a dramatic interpretation competition. She went on to win an oratory contest that ultimately secured a full-ride scholarship to Tennessee State University. At Tennessee State she studied communications. And more doors opened. At the age of seventeen she became Miss Black Tennessee. This notoriety attracted media attention which turned into her first break in broadcasting.

After graduating from college Oprah quickly moved up within the media ranks. She became a newscaster and then ultimately a talk show host. By her early thirties she was

Chapter 10: Relationships Make or Break

hosting the nationally syndicated Oprah Winfrey Show. During a run of twenty-five years at the top of the ratings Oprah built her own media dynasty. She became a billionaire, the wealthiest self-made woman in the world.

By every objective measure Oprah had few advantages and a seemingly endless supply of disadvantages. She didn't come from a stable, secure family. She didn't have a well-connected inner circle to open doors for her. She didn't have access to an Ivy League education. She had to rely on her talents and determination, and the good graces and guidance and support of people she met along the way. She built and nurtured relationships that strengthened her, that helped her advance. Those relationships helped Oprah succeed spectacularly.

I'll give you, Oprah is uniquely talented. She has special gifts that set her apart, that's true. But so do you.

You have unique gifts and talents. You have a unique opportunity and a unique purpose; a mission to complete during your lifetime on this earth. You have a special contribution to make to life that no one else can make.

No one would have expected much from young Oprah. Observers would have determined that she would wallow in poverty for a short and troubled existence. Her lot was cast. But Oprah saw something else. Other people saw it too and were there for her.

Because she kept going, because she kept moving forward with hope in her heart, doors opened and circumstances changed. When she recognized opportunity

Chapter 10: Relationships Make or Break

she remade herself, she changed her habits and instead of moving from trial to tragedy she moved on to uncommon triumph.

What about you?

What do you see?

Do you see opportunity or is your vision clouded?

Oprah leveraged her strengths. She buckled down and ultimately developed her version of high performance habits – habits to carry her to new heights. She built a network of support.

Oprah was not immune to life's demons and insecurities. She faced then, and still faces today, anxiety and fear – like we all do. But, Oprah chooses to move forward. Oprah chooses to make the most of what she has.

What do you choose?

Oprah expressed her gifts connecting with other people. She built her fortune communicating with, educating and inspiring others. People around the world respond to Oprah's giving – giving of herself, her vulnerability, her curiosity, her capacity to love. Oprah listened to her grandmother; she found her voice and she uses it.

Uncover your talents and nurture them.

You have greatness within you. Let that greatness out!

Make expressing your gifts a habit. Other people are waiting to help.

Chapter 11
It's All About Relationships

If it is true, 'We're here to help others,' what exactly then are the others here for?

Shouldn't they be here for us – to help us?

A Course in Miracles states, "It takes great learning to understand that all things, events, encounters and circumstances are helpful." If all those people sharing our lives don't seem to be helping, if all those people we encounter on the highways and byways, in the hustle and bustle of life seem more of a hindrance than a help, maybe we need to consider we're just not seeing the big picture, we aren't grasping the entire truth.

As the population expands opportunities are multiplying. More people, more chances to connect, to give, to grow, to learn, to create, to love.

We are not alone. We are not traveling alone. Life is a collective journey. We need people and people need us.

Each individual has strengths and weaknesses, special gifts and talents. We are stronger, more intelligent, and more capable together than we can possibly be alone. We encourage each other, we inspire each other, and we support each other.

Life is all about relationships.

Chapter 11: It's All About Relationships

In this section, **Part 3** and the previous section, **Part 2**, we focus on those few key habits that give us the most leverage in life; the habits that allow us to perform up to our potential. We are exploring high performance habits.

We've highlighted attitude and mindset. We've explored the power of building confidence. Now we turn our attention to the collective – to relationships.

We are meant to be operating on our default setting; a setting where we are connected, safe and secure, confident and capable, excited and optimistic. We are meant to be performing at an extremely high level, but since we encountered the weight and resistance of the environment we often lose our way. We fumble around in the dark. And in the dark, we allow fear to dominate. We throw the switch. Instead of empowering optimum performance, we settle. We determine just getting by is good enough. Anything else isn't worth the effort; isn't worth the risk.

So far in *High Performance Habits* we've explored the lives of three remarkable individuals: Oprah Winfrey, Thomas Edison, and Andrew Carnegie. These three overcame monumental challenges to realize extraordinary accomplishments. Each of them took advantage of opportunities that led down exciting, demanding, prosperous paths. But, you know what? All the opportunities that came to Oprah and Edison and Carnegie came by way of other people; no exceptions.

Inspiration comes from the *Source*, but more often than not, it is delivered by way of other people. We are guided

Chapter 11: It's All About Relationships

by, encouraged by, inspired by, and supported by, other people.

How we manage relationships; how we develop and nurture interpersonal skills; our social habits matter. They matter a great deal.

Once we are in this jungle of time and space it's easy to fall victim to fear. It's easy to begin to believe we're lost, separate and alone. If we believe we have some skills, some talent, and some power we'll buckle down to compete – to take what we want. If we don't believe we have skills and talent and power we will scurry around looking for the safest place to hide. It, this journey of life, will eventually be over anyway.

There are two primary ways to sustain and empower our default setting. The first is by way of our personal motivation; our attitude and mindset. When we've got these right we are connected and driven; not driven to compete and dominate, but rather driven to explore and experience, to express more life, to fulfill our potential. With the right attitude and mindset we are focused and capable of traveling fast.

The second way to sustain and empower our default setting also happens to be the most common means of impeding progress; of switching us from our default to a base setting. It's the people around us; our social support network. We are influenced, for better or for worse, for

Chapter 11: It's All About Relationships

richer, for poorer, by the people in our lives, from the very beginning.

The people that have surrounded us have influenced who we have become. They have influenced our core beliefs – the beliefs that determine what manifests in our lives.

Regardless of the environments you have endured and the nature of your support system up to this point, take stock of where you are now.

Are you surrounded by confident, positive people, people who see opportunity, are willing to grow, and are going somewhere?

Do you have a network of positive, supportive people to help you advance, grow and become?

High performers deliberately associate with and surround themselves with positive, uplifting, capable people. High performers put forth focused effort when it comes to building and maintaining relationships.

It's time to conduct another inventory.

You've already compiled your **Habits Inventory** and you've compared your habits to the habits high performers employ. Now we have to confront the brutal facts. Are you surrounded by people that are helping you achieve your potential or by people that are holding you back?

Make a list of the all the people you associate with: family members (immediate and extended); friends and

Chapter 11: It's All About Relationships

acquaintances; co-workers, employees and employers; and other people you interact with routinely. This will be your **Associates Inventory**.

Before you go further, remember this point: I am going to ask you to make an assessment of each individual. We tend to think our judgment is objective. It can't be objective. Remember that your assessment of anyone and anything, of everyone and everything, is the result of your perspective and biases. In other words, your assessment may not be accurate. Accept this fact. It will only help in the long run.

Next to each person you listed on your **Associates Inventory** put a plus (+) if you believe they are a positive influence, an uplifting support in your life. Put a dash (–) if you believe they are a negative influence, an inhibiting force to your progress. And put a slash (/) if you determine they are on balance neutral, that is neither usually positive nor usually negative.

Now count up your pluses and minuses. How does your inventory look? Are you associating with the right kind of people?

Before you start down the path of judging people and ending relationships consider this. What we see in other people is often a reflection of ourselves. So reconsider the people you have cataloged in the negative column. How do you routinely present yourself to these people? The problem is not necessarily them. If we are honest with ourselves the problem may be us.

Chapter 11: It's All About Relationships

Once you have done that work, you should have a macro picture of whether or not you have a positive, life-enhancing support network.

If you don't have a supportive, inspiring network, it's time to establish a network-building, a relationship-building habit.

If you want to go somewhere – if you want to have more, do more and become more – you have to surround yourself with, routinely associate with, positive, growth-minded, and uplifting people.

Positive, growth-minded people will help you keep a positive attitude and stay in a growth mindset. Positive, growth-minded people will help you see opportunities and encourage you to take risks to get out of your comfort zone, try new things, and explore new places and grow.

The right support network of people will push you, will challenge you, will test you. If you truly want to be a high performer you will respond to the challenge. You will get out of your comfort zone and you will get on the trail of growth.

It's not about the number of people you have on your team. It's about the quality of the people you have on your team and the mutual bond of trust and respect between team members.

Altering the course of your relationships may prove to be the most difficult habit to change in this entire process of

Chapter 11: It's All About Relationships

developing high performance habits. But nothing, no change of habits that you make is going to prove to be more rewarding.

What we are talking about here, is potentially changing the collection of people you associate with in all areas of your life except for one. You owe it to your family and friends - to the people who are closest to you – to evolve the nature of your current relationship. If the relationship is on balance negative, that is has a negative influence on you, than your task is to change yourself and start bringing something more positive to the relationship. With children this is one hundred percent, your responsibility. With adults, reforming a negative relationship is going to take work and ultimately cooperation from both people involved.

Leaving negative people behind, doesn't mean you shut them out. Family is family. Your task in dealing with negative people is to bring positive energy to bear. Bring positive energy to the relationship. If some people are unwilling or unable to absorb your positive energy they will tend to avoid you.

The high performance habit here is to associate with and surround yourself with positive, growth-minded people. The place to begin this process is by changing your habit of mind, so that you exhibit a positive attitude and a growth mindset. Once you have this habit of mind, you will naturally gravitate toward like-minded people. You will start reforming and refreshing your network.

Chapter 11: It's All About Relationships

Then take the process one step further. Make the act of connecting with and interacting with positive, growth-minded people a habit. You will be better for it.

In the next chapter we are going to focus more specifically on communication habits. These are the skills we use to nurture relationships. Few skills are more important or more valuable.

If we want to be high performers we must learn to communicate positively and effectively.

Succeeding, success is all about relationships. Start nurturing yours.

Chapter 12
Are We Communicating?

Have you ever had trouble being understood?

Have you ever had trouble getting your message across?

When traveling to a place where the native language is not my own, my first response after making a statement or asking a question that clearly was not understood, is to repeat myself. Only this time I say it louder.

It's a quite natural, well let's not say natural, let's say a typical human reaction to judge someone who doesn't understand you as less intelligent. Why clearly, what I was saying made perfect sense. I even applied necessary tonal inflections and appropriate body language.

Might we consider, it could be the transmitter that is failing; not the receiver?

If you are in a foreign country and you are judging someone who doesn't speak your language as somehow lacking, how do you suppose they are judging you?

Closer to home we do the same thing with our loved ones. If they, our family, friends, co-workers, customers, acquaintances, don't understand us, something must be wrong with them.

What we often determine to be communication is really just transmission.

Chapter 12: Are We Communicating?

Most often what we intend to serve as communication is really a demand. For instance, with our children, "Hey, take that ball and go outside."

As is typical, we immediately perceive a lack of compliance with our demand and up goes the volume. The intention doesn't change, but now the effort we must exert shortens the message, "Ball, outside. Now!"

If the kids comply, we rejoice, we've communicated. Our demand has been met. Our command has been complied with. If not, if those annoying young ones ignore our demand or worse, resist, we generally up the ante, "If you don't take that ball outside this instant…" And to really ensure our message gets through we add a limited gesture, or for full force, a total body gesture.

Ah, mission accomplished.

We do this with the most special and the most important people in our lives. Poor communications habits, like a tendency to transmit as a means of communication, infects every one of our relationships. We think, from our own perspective that we deliver a clear, common sense, reasonable intention, and at times we are met with silence, a muted response signaling distraction, a misinterpretation, or sometimes, usually at the most inopportune of times, downright opposition.

If this strikes home in the least, just what the heck is going on with our communication habits?

Chapter 12: Are We Communicating?

After mindset, the most important high performance habit to develop is the habit of building, nurturing, and sustaining positive productive relationships. The ability to communicate effectively may be, is arguably, the most important skill a human being can master.

Why do we struggle with it, why do we struggle with communication so?

Why do we employ poor communication habits even with the people closest to us – the very people who should understand us best?

Each of us has various notions about this concept of communication. And many, if not most of our ideas are wrong. Attitude and mindset, confidence and self-esteem, power and control are all wrapped up in relationships and therefore must always be considerations when communicating.

Because of lifelong conditioning communicators normally assume one of three roles in trying to get a message across, to ultimately achieve an objective. Two of these three roles are complementary. Usually if one person approaches a communication in one of these roles the other person falls into the opposite or opposing role. These two roles I'm talking about are parent – child.

If someone approaches a communication whining, complaining and demonstrating an unwillingness to take responsibility, that person is assuming a child role. The

Chapter 12: Are We Communicating?

typical response to a whining child is to assume the role of controlling parent. As you can imagine, automatically falling into these roles is not a recipe for successful communication.

The third and most productive of our three communication roles is the one for effective, productive communication. That is an equal adult role. The equal adult role assumes no status, no power position, and fosters genuine, candid, non-judgmental communication.

Do you have a habit of falling into either the parent or child role when you communicate with certain people?

Watch for this habit. Ask someone you trust if you do that – if you automatically assume a child or controlling parent demeanor with some people or in certain circumstances.

Falling into either a child or controlling parent role is a habit to break.

We start out early making the mistake, equating the ability to speak with the ability to communicate. Don't get me wrong, learning to speak greatly enhances our options to communicate, but speaking is no panacea.

New parents spend the first two years of their child's life trying to get them to walk and to talk – to speak. Usually they succeed to such a degree they devote the next sixteen years to trying to get these very same children to sit down and shut up.

Chapter 12: Are We Communicating?

Once the communication fuse is lit, that is once we learn that we can convey to others what we think in our heads and feel in our hearts, there is no turning us off. We validate our thoughts, our feelings, yes our very existence by means of relating to, and communicating with other people. Unfortunately we don't always relate well.

Like in virtually everything else, we establish communication shortcuts. We develop and nurture communication habits – many of which get in our way. Bad communication habits limit our ability to connect and ultimately limit our ability to advance and succeed.

George Bernard Shaw pointed out, "The single biggest problem with communication is the illusion it has taken place."

You know this is true, because we all experience this every day in our closest and most intimate relationships – in our interactions with family members and friends. The great skill of communication is often subjugated to a more urgent need – whatever has our attention.

Just think about that ceaseless babbling of a talkative five year old. Or the self-involved banter of the insecure teenager. Or the emotion laden convictions of a spouse painstakingly instructing you on the right way to do something you are most comfortable with doing your own way. Can you relate?

The communication habits we learn to employ in circumstances like these are rarely productive. Rather in these circumstances most often we employ filters to block

Chapter 12: Are We Communicating?

out what we perceive to be useless noise. Or we rely on self-restraint to keep the peace and get through the exchange.

Connecting with positive, growth-minded people is essential for our personal development. Modeling positive, growth-minded behavior is essential for teaching and supporting children. But, with the wrong communication habits we crush opportunities to validate others; to confirm their value to us, to communicate and connect.

We have work to do.

Looking at your **Habits Inventory**, how many communications related habits have you already discovered and cataloged?

Are the habits you have listed helpful or hurtful? Do they foster or inhibit connections and growth?

Before engaging in any communication, keep this in mind. Every communication consists of two components: **the relationship** and **the message**. The relationship is inherently valuable and its potential extends far beyond the explicit message or immediate exchange. And remember, the message itself consists of symbols; words, tones, facial expressions and gestures; that each can be interpreted multiple ways. Eighty percent of communication is nonverbal. Don't get lost in the words and by all means don't jump to conclusions.

Seek to understand before seeking to be understood. Only then are you fostering genuine communication.

Chapter 12: Are We Communicating?

Always make the relationship the priority; the specific message is always secondary.

The process of communication is a loop – a cycle.

An idea is conveyed via some means: words, sounds, gestures, in writing, through a telephone, by means of text or email or smoke signals for that matter, a nearly endless variety. The transmission, the expression, is where most of us stop. We think by saying a word, or making a gesture, or sending an email, we have communicated. This is the illusion of communication.

For communication to take place we must complete the cycle – close the loop. The person being communicated with must receive the idea, the expression, by whatever means. They must absorb it, not ignore in, and then they must interpret what they received. At this point the communicator has expressed a message, but the process is not done yet – the loop is not closed.

A message has been transmitted, received and interpreted. Now the communicator will get feedback as to what the receiver interpreted and intends. Communication doesn't happen until the loop is all the way closed.

This communication process is one fraught with opportunity for failure.

Just think if your communication habits are not working to facilitate this entire process. Your attempts at communication will fail, and you will fail to connect.

Chapter 12: Are We Communicating?

Skeptics say that human beings invented language to satisfy our deepest, most heartfelt urge – that is our need to complain. By and large, people use language as a tool for concealing the truth; and this doesn't help us connect. And while skeptics have a point, and we do use language often as a veil to conceal our true intent, our ability to communicate, our ability to connect, is what has allowed us to survive and thrive in an increasingly complex and challenging world.

If you want to perform at a high level, if you want to succeed in our fast-paced, rapidly-changing, supercharged world, and by succeed I mean have money, have friends, and actually have the time to enjoy both, you have to develop effective communication habits.

I'd like to make a recommendation here. Pick up and read ***How to Win Friends and Influence People*** by Dale Carnegie. In this single illuminating volume you will likely discover two things. First, you'll uncover bad communication habits that you may not have yet cataloged. Things like a tendency to condemn, criticize and complain; or poor listening habits. And second, you'll learn the keys to effective, relationship-building communication.

Communication is a life-enhancing skill that we work on over the course of a lifetime.

You can't go wrong, choosing and developing effective communication habits.

Chapter 12: Are We Communicating?

We communicate to connect. So if we want to succeed – if we want to be high performers – we must develop the right communication habits.

In the next chapter, chapter 13, we are going to take a look at relationships from a broader perspective. We'll explore the power of cultural habits. We'll see how important it is to run with the right crowd.

Chapter 13
Running with the Right Crowd

At this point in our high performance habits journey I hope you think we are making good progress. We have come a long way, covered a lot of ground.

We have recognized the power of habit – habits dominate our lives.

Habits can significantly impede our progress, or if we develop high performance habits, habits can greatly accelerate our advance; our success in life. We have explored the habit loop and determined not all habits are equal. Some habits serve as levers exerting vast influence.

Fostering the right high performance habits makes a huge difference.

We have looked specifically at some high performance habits, the ones that determine whether individuals fly high – travel far and fast – or whether individuals tune out and settle in. Among the high performance habits are getting your mindset right, fine-tuning and employing your body, and building and maintaining a positive, supportive network.

Here now we are going to explore another function or display of habits. Habits are not just a trait of individuals. Habits are tools of the collective.

Families develop and nurture habits. Groups of friends operate by, or settle into habits; habitual ways of interacting.

Chapter 13: Running with the Right Crowd

Remember the purpose of a habit is to allow us to employ minimal effort to achieve a sought after reward.

Workplaces, organizations, associations, all develop habits. We usually recognize and label these collections of habits, an organization's culture.

As you know, and as we have stressed throughout this book, we are individuals, but we are greatly influenced by other people. We are connected, like it or not.

To chart our best course, to foster our own growth, and to maintain the path to where we want to go, we must be aware of the cultures we immerse ourselves in, the groups we associate with, the crowds we run with.

The influence of collective or organizational habits is profound. And just like in personal relationships we have to both police our own motives and conduct, and diligently and deliberately select those environments – the cultures – we operate in. Family cultures, group cultures, workplace cultures, influence us. And we contribute to these cultures.

I should mention here though again, we are not victims. We contribute to, we nurture, and we reinforce family, group and organizational cultures. Just like the personal habits we have developed and employ routinely throughout all areas of our lives, we have direct responsibility for and control over some cultures, like family. And we are responsible for choosing the cultures we operate in and allow to influence us.

Chapter 13: Running with the Right Crowd

We possess both the power and the ultimate responsibility when it comes to the management of our lives. We are in control. We have the power. ***High Performance Habits***, this book, is all about putting that power to the best use.

Here's a question for you: Why do you work?

I know I, and I suspect most people, answer the question, 'Why work?' to get money, to support ourselves, pay the bills, and maintain a lifestyle. We work to get.

It seems an odd notion, but working to get does conform to the laws of life. We have to put forth effort to get a reward, and in the case of work, for most people, this means trading hours of time, energy and effort for a paycheck.

It may be the nature of the word work; that the word itself carries a negative connotation, much like the words labor and toil. We automatically associate these words with effort, and usually effort that is prescribed; that is, beyond our control. This perceived lack of autonomy, of self-direction, associated with work, our jobs, is the primary reason so many people dislike what they do. This limited perspective is just that – limited.

An enlightened perspective will see that we are still in control and responsible. It is up to us to make choices, to choose where we devote our efforts and why. It is up to us to make the best of our circumstance; to do the best we can with what we've got.

Chapter 13: Running with the Right Crowd

Of course that's easy to say, "Take responsibility for your life." The reality is usually more complex. The tapestry, the influences and the rhythm of life are far more subtle. Sometimes we are just not sure who is in control. Typically the way life works is we only put out effort to get something in return. Every cause has an effect. Every action has an equal and opposite reaction. Nothing is done in a vacuum. All action produces a result; a conscious sought after result or an unconscious one. Life is motion, action; that's just the way it is. It is easy to see how sometimes, and for some people, most of the time, things get out of control.

Back to our question of "Why work?" In the case of work, putting out effort for something translates into time and energy offered in return for a paycheck or a payoff of some sort for our labor.

If money wasn't an object do you think you would work?

We all want to be in the leisure class. We would like to have enough money and resources to be able to spend our days in idle pursuits. If we have enough money we can do anything we want with our time. Sounds pretty good doesn't it?

Let's consider this notion of work from another perspective.

What is work after all? It's a process, an activity, that requires a degree of focus and concentration. Work requires

Chapter 13: Running with the Right Crowd

our energy and attention. But what exactly are we doing when we work?

Why we are adding value. We are adding value to someone else's life. We are adding value to this world. Work is really a means to create more life. Through work we serve, we create, we give. Unfortunately most of us only focus on getting.

Wouldn't you love to devote yourself to a vocation that excites you every day; something that makes you want to get out of bed in the morning and get going?

Wouldn't it be awesome to be committed to a task that is larger than yourself, a task that you share with a team of positive, highly motivated and committed people, a task that is contributing immense value to the world?

If you found such an activity; if you found yourself working in an energetic, exciting place making a valuable contribution, do you think money would be your highest motive?

Back to that question of: Why do you work?

Let's leave the getting part behind. You work to add value to people's lives. You work to create more life.

Isn't that purpose enough?

Chapter 13: Running with the Right Crowd

Can you imagine being in a work environment with a culture devoted to a cause, electric with excitement and overflowing with enthusiasm?

Wouldn't this be a great place to work?

Wouldn't this be a magnificent creative outlet?

Why isn't your workplace like this?

The lives we lead, our personal lives, our lives with our family and friends, our professional lives, and our public lives are all dominated by habits. Every working establishment, the atmosphere, the environment, is a product of habits – primarily habits of the people in leadership positions – but also cultural habits that have developed cooperatively over time.

The organization, the team, the people, establish ways of doing things, ways of dealing with each other, customers, clients, suppliers and vendors, and ways of dealing with those outside the group. If you can recognize these organizational habits, good and bad, you can begin to influence habit formation and ultimately organizational performance. You can influence the cultures of the groups where you spend the greatest concentration of your time, energy and effort.

The same collection of high performance habits ensures the well-being of families, teams, and organizations of all sorts.

Chapter 13: Running with the Right Crowd

Attitude and mindset are essential. The culture must be positive and growth oriented – focused on adding value and creating, not competing.

Health and vitality matter. The culture must value individuals: their intellects, their insights, their contributions and their health and well-being.

Associations matter here too. High performing teams and organizations link with like-minded organizations to reinforce the growth mindset.

And high performing cultures are focused and disciplined. High performing cultures have a mission and purpose. The people in these organizations are committed to their mission and to the other people on the team. They give their personal efforts so that collectively those efforts are multiplied and the organization can create.

The power of a team, focused, committed, and disciplined, is awesome.

Recognizing group and organizations' cultural habits allows you to make more informed choices about your associations, about your roles, and about your leadership. Leadership in a family, on a team, in an association or a workplace is critical.

Remember we talked about: 'You get what you give.' People respond to and reflect back the energy you transmit, positive or negative. If you always transmit positive energy, even in the face of negative energy from others, you are choosing to lead and lead productively.

Chapter 13: Running with the Right Crowd

Choose to lead and choose to invest your time, your energy and your talents in organizations that reinforce growth; in organizations and with teams that truly add maximum value for the effort committed.

I have another task for you. This time you're going to conduct an audit of three key organizations: your immediate family, your workplace organization, and at least one other group or organization you routinely associate with. This could be your extended family, a place of worship, or even a favorite business you frequent.

You are going to conduct a **Cultural Habits Inventory**. This inventory will identify and catalog collective habits of your family, your place of employment and at least one other group. You will be assessing the nature of the cultures of groups you associate with.

Much like you did when conducting your own habits inventory, identify and compile a list of "habits" or group norms you observe in each of three collective settings. How do family or group members greet each other? How do they interact? Are there routine ways of doing things? Do members of the group follow definite prescribed or loosely developed processes to relate to each other and to achieve group objectives?

The lists of habits you compile here do not have to be exhaustive or comprehensive. You will have to separate yourself somewhat from the routines of the organization, family or group, to be able to recognize the collective habits

Chapter 13: Running with the Right Crowd

that have developed and that are being employed. Once you've listed various habits, enough so that you feel like you have a good sense of the organization, assess whether or not you think each of the habits, norms of behavior or processes used by group members, are positive and growth-oriented or not. Consider each collective habit. Is it a process that builds people up or tears people down? Is it a process that helps people connect or is it a process that alienates individuals? Is it a process that helps people learn and grow or is it a process that stifles creativity and inhibits contribution?

If you are seeing more negative than positive, you have identified a negative culture. A negative culture inhibits growth and stifles creativity. This is not an environment that nourishes high performers.

Next consider how much you are responsible for the habits the group exhibits.

Do you think you should be working to change some cultural habits here?

Do you think perhaps you should be looking for other associations as these cultures are not serving you?

Collective habits, family norms, and organizational cultures matter. High performers ensure that the environments they frequent actively support their cause: their growth, their development, and ultimately their overall happiness and success. Choose carefully the groups and organizations you associate with. Run with the right crowd.

Chapter 13: Running with the Right Crowd

Through ***High Performance Habits*** so far, we've examined the power of habits. We've discussed choosing the right habits and surveyed the key habits that provide the most leverage for success.

In the next and final section, **Part 4**, we are going to get on with the task of changing habits. We are going to start adopting high performance habits.

Let's get going.

Part 4

Making Success a Habit

Chapter 14
Walk by Faith

Have you ever attempted or completed something physically challenging?

Would you like to? Say something like running a Spartan Race or a Tough Mudder?

How about running a marathon?

Or taking it up a notch, completing an Iron Man triathlon or one of those extreme endurance races of 50 to 100 miles or more?

Have you, or have you ever thought about climbing a mountain; one of the bigger ones, Denali, K2, Everest?

How about hiking the Appalachian Trail? That's a trail that stretches from Maine to Georgia over 2,100 miles.

Do you think you would be up for the challenge; a through hike on the Appalachian Trail? That is starting at one end and hiking to the other, from start to finish in one go.

A few thousand people start the hike every year intending to negotiate the length of the entire Appalachian Trail. Typically a few hundred complete the trek.

Do you think it would be easier and more manageable to hike with a group for support and camaraderie? What about going it alone?

Chapter 14: Walk by Faith

Now I'll add one degree of difficulty for you to consider. Would you be up for the challenge if you were blind?

In 1990 Bill Irwin, a blind 50-year-old medical technologist and his German Shepherd guide dog, Orient, began the treacherous journey of navigating the Appalachian Trail at Springer Mountain in Georgia. They headed north into the wilderness. It was raining.

Bill and Orient didn't have maps, or a compass, or a GPS navigation system. As Bill put it, "He traveled by faith, not by sight."

Neither Bill nor Orient were experienced mountaineers. They were rookies, greenhorns, complete novices. They attempted to do something that had never been done before. They both learned and changed and grew from the challenge. They never quit.

Bill did not know it at the time, that day he took his first step along the "AT" as the Appalachian Trail is affectionately known, but he would risk his and Orient's life numerous times to complete that grueling trek.

Bill's life would never be the same. Bill would never be the same. That hike was his salvation.

Bill wasn't looking for an adventure. Truth be told he had lived a troubled life. He had had four failed marriages and had been an absentee father to three children by his first wife. Most of his adult years he was an alcoholic.

Chapter 14: Walk by Faith

Things hadn't begun poorly for Bill. After a quick start out of college, for whatever reasons, life's challenges began to add up and Bill's life experiences gradually drifted down. Bill graduated from Samford University in Birmingham, Alabama with a bachelor's degree in chemistry and biology in 1964. Within a couple of years of graduation he founded a lab business that he built into quite a success.

When Bill was only twenty-eight however, a worsening eye problem was misdiagnosed as cancer. Doctors removed his left eye. By the age of thirty-six he was completely blind. While he focused on sustaining his professional life Bill's personal life floundered. He felt lost and grew resentful. He drank more. He smoked five packs of cigarettes a day. Almost as if without his knowing it Bill gradually developed habits that destroyed rather than lifted up.

Like most alcoholics Bill denied he had a problem until he was forced to confront his demons. He agreed to accompany and support his son through a week-long inpatient substance-abuse treatment program to combat his son's cocaine addiction. Attempting to survive the week without a drink, agonizingly for himself and the staff of the treatment center, made it painfully clear to Bill he was an alcoholic. He decided then and there to change course.

By 1987 with the help of his newly developed devotion to Christ Bill was sober. Over the course of the next few years "coincidences" converged guiding him to attempt to hike the AT.

Chapter 14: Walk by Faith

While many hikers entertain a romantic notion of freedom and adventure on the trail Bill approached his trek as a mission, as work. He never considered or expected the 2,100 mile hike to be fun; most hikers quit when it's not fun anymore. Bill just knew hiking the AT was something he had to do. Quitting was not an option.

Bill and Orient began their trek in a driving rain. Ahead of them lie struggles with navigation, food and water, heat and cold, sharp rocks, swollen rivers, towering mountains and steep cliffs.

Imagine the challenges they faced. Think of how you would negotiate all those obstacles, all those ascents and descents, fallen trees and swathes of washed out trail; then think about doing it blind.

Bill and Orient had to learn, nurture and develop a new set of habits – habits to ensure they could survive and ultimately thrive on the 2,100 mile quest. Immediately navigation proved a problem. Bill couldn't see the colored hash marks delineating the trail and Orient didn't know what they meant. After repeated trial and error, with the aid of other hikers, and over the course of months Orient learned to track the scent of through-hikers. He even eventually learned to distinguish the trail markers. Orient became so good at navigating the trail that other hikers began to rely on him to keep them straight.

By Bill's recollection eighty percent of the time hiking conditions were less than optimal. It was raining or snowing, too hot or too cold. Bill and Orient both had to get

Chapter 14: Walk by Faith

used to dealing with the elements and the pace of daily trekking. A dog is not naturally adept at or ready for long hours of work. Gradually however, Orient adapted to the unrelenting grind. As a matter of fact, Bill said the longer they were out on the trail the stronger Orient got, while Bill's body began to breakdown. Where Bill encouraged Orient to begin the journey Orient encouraged Bill to complete the passage.

Along one stretch of the trail, through Pennsylvania, the rocks are known to be quite treacherous. Hikers joke that the locals come through and sharpen the rocks for fun. Bill had brought leather pads for Orient but they proved to be too restrictive. The trail tore up Orient's paws. So much so, that Bill and Orient had to take a week off from hiking to allow Orient to heal.

Bill estimated he fell thousands of times along the way. No matter how hard the fall, Bill's task was always the same: to get back up. He was scratched and bruised. He even cracked his ribs. He suffered from heat exhaustion in the south and hypothermia in the north. But he kept on going.

The "Orient Express" as the pair were called, traversed New England in October and November. At swollen rivers Bill would release Orient who would then negotiate the river on his own. Once safe on the other side Orient would call out to Bill by means of barks and whines to help him pass through the water. It's a miracle they both survived.

Some eight months after setting out from Springer Mountain, Georgia, Bill and Orient reached the terminus of

Chapter 14: Walk by Faith

the Appalachian Trail at Mount Katahdin in Maine. Along the way Bill had arranged for the delivery of over 500 personalized copies of *Bibles*. He sent *Bibles* to young people he encountered and encouraged along the way.

The Orient Express faced daunting, life threatening challenges, but when things seemed at their worst someone or some kindly group was always on hand to provide what was needed and help salvage the situation. In truth Bill and Orient were never alone.

Bill's confidence in his and Orient's ability to succeed was vested in his faith in a power beyond himself – a power that guided and reassured. Bill and Orient's disciplined habits and dogged determination (just had to do it) saw them through a challenge most sighted people would never attempt.

The Orient Express was a team built on a foundation of faith – connected to the *Source*. That team executed high performance habits to answer a call and share a story of wonder and hope, and comfort and joy, along a trail of trial and discomfort.

Bill Irwin proved that armed with a little faith it is possible to develop the right habits to achieve the impossible.

A little faith will take you a long way.

Chapter 15
Cultivating Habits

We are at the point in our journey together where we are going to move beyond theory and jump into action. To change direction we actually have to do something.

I know, I know one of two things probably ran through your mind when you read these words, "do something."

Hopefully you were energized and excited, thinking:

"It's about time. What can we do? Let's get going fast out of the gate."

Or, you went immediately into denial.

"My life's not that bad. Things are pretty good, at least tolerable. My habits are really not hindering me."

If you are resisting the idea of real and lasting change; of putting forth some effort to change your habits, you have probably run up against your "terror barrier." Your terror barrier is that protective wall you have built and maintained over your lifetime to protect your self: your core beliefs – about this world, who you are, and about your place in it.

It seems the only thing people like better than the ways things are, is the way things were. Even though everything about this life is in motion, that is, changing, too many people cling to whatever advantage, comfort, or status they have.

Chapter 15: Cultivating Habits

In the next chapter we will deal specifically with overcoming fear and resistance to change. Here we lay out a process to deliberately identify and replace habits that are not serving us with habits that do serve us – high performance habits.

Here's the process in a nutshell: determine where you want to go; make a plan to get there; and then act. It's all very simple really.

You can work through this process using the ***High Performance Habits'*** **Habits Change Process** (Appendix B). Create your own worksheet or pick up an electronic version in the ***High Performance Habits*** online program, and put pen to paper.

So let's begin. Shall we?

What's our starting point?

Our starting point is a gut check. We have got to measure desire. Desire is the starting point of all achievement. Desire is our motivation to act.

You have to answer this question:

"Do I really want to change?"

Do you really want to change?

Truthfully answering that question is your starting point.

Chapter 15: Cultivating Habits

Lukewarm desire produces lukewarm results. You'll likely make some progress, but permanent change is doubtful.

Real and lasting change is fueled by real and lasting motivation. You have to want to change. You've got to want to leave the path you are on and instead start moving down a new path, toward a new worthwhile destination.

I know you are anxious to get to the how of change. But until you have settled on a "WHY" that really and truly moves you, the how is inconsequential.

Once you are motivated to change, the next step is fostering a belief that change is possible. At this point this belief in your ability to change doesn't even need to be your belief. Someone else believing in you, believing you can change, is good enough.

The state you want to nurture, the feeling you want to reinforce I believe is best described by the word anticipation. You want to be excited and expectant; this is the state of anticipation. You are moving toward something and anticipating that experience you are moving toward. You believe it is possible, more than that; you know it is likely. It's just right there…

I can tell you, without question you have what it takes to change. You have unimaginable potential. All you have to do to begin realizing that potential is to take a step in a new direction. Are you ready?

Chapter 15: Cultivating Habits

Okay, the only answer that is keeping you with me is yes. Yes you want to change.

Let me suggest, the first habit you might want to develop is a habit to fuel desire.

Fashion some sort of reminder that will trigger a ritual you can build into a habit; something that will continually rekindle your desire. To succeed you need to keep revisiting that state of anticipation.

You know what is going to happen, like has happened so many times before? You get excited about a new prospect. You get all fired up and ready to take on the world when an obstacle springs up. The strain of the effort takes its toll. Soon that fire of desire is at risk of being doused.

In those moments, remember Bill Irwin's thought process. He wasn't hiking the Appalachian Trail to have fun. He was hiking the 2,100 miles, stumbling and falling, struggling and losing his way, to do what he had to do. He never for a moment thought that he was hiking for fun. It was effort, it was uncomfortable, and at times it was painful. But no matter what, Bill had only one thing to do: move; and only one way to go: forward.

You must keep your desire burning. Make a habit that will fire that level of excitement and enthusiasm quickly and easily – that state of joyous, grateful, anticipation.

The starting point of all achievement, the starting point of all change is desire.

Chapter 15: Cultivating Habits

Spend however long it takes; igniting a burning desire. That desire will see you through the dark and lonely times of trial. And don't kid yourself, there will be moments of trial along the way. Plan for them. Plan to stumble, plan to fall, but plan always to get up and keep going.

You need to have a clear vision of where you want to go. We move toward what we focus on. Establish a clear and definite goal. Make a habit of focusing on that goal and reminding yourself why.

Now it is time to confront the brutal facts.

Look again at your **Habits Inventory**.

Identify which habits are working for you and which habits are working against you.

Over time you are going to eliminate your bad habits by replacing them with good habits. Eliminating bad habits will significantly improve your life, but if you want to become a high performer, deliberately develop high performing habits in place of your bad habits.

Some habits are easier to change than others. Some will only take a few days to reset, others will take months. Like deleting something on your computer, the access is cut but the data is still there, the old habit pattern will virtually always exist; it's not gone.

We are always susceptible to falling back into old habit patterns. Recognize when you are falling back into past habit patterns. When you see this happening; when you

Chapter 15: Cultivating Habits

realize you are falling into an old, bad habit pattern act to redirect yourself.

How does your list look? Do you only have a few habits that need to change or do you need a total makeover?

Prioritize the first few habits you are going to replace. Changing habits works best if you focus on one habit at a time; so pick the first habit to change.

Work one habit at a time, step by step. At first you may feel impatient as this change process will seem very time consuming. Relax. Consistent small steps in the right direction are much more productive than hurried or harried steps in the wrong direction. You've got a lifetime to change. Trust you will progress.

Make a plan. Write it out.

Carefully complete every component of the ***Habits Change Process*** worksheet. Ultimately you will work through a number of habits, but for now focus on one habit at a time.

Sketch out the habit loop for the bad habit – that habit you intend to replace. This is often not a simple task. Many of the triggers, the cues, can be unconscious or are not very obvious. You may have to devote some time to detective work here.

Chapter 15: Cultivating Habits

What is the stimulus, the cue, the trigger that gets this habit rolling? What desire or craving does the cue evoke?

We human beings are exceptional rationalizers. We often, usually, mostly always fabricate reasons for our actions after the fact. Be clear on what is driving you to act.

Let's say you snack late at night routinely. You might be watching TV and soon find yourself heading for the refrigerator. An easy association might be: watching television triggers hunger. However, the real motivation may be that you are lonely or bored. Figuring out the trigger, what it is you really crave, is going to take some soul searching.

The physical routine is usually the easiest part of the habit cycle to map out. In an action habit it is a matter of chronicling what exactly you do in your routine. Thought and feeling habits are a little more involved and require some emotional maturity and intellectual honesty to decipher and dissect. With some work you can define what rabbit hole your mind runs down or what feelings rise to the surface when you confront a given trigger. Sort these out carefully.

Next determine the reward you are after in that habit routine.

Sketch out the entire habit cycle. This is going to pay dividends as you work through the habits change process.

Chapter 15: Cultivating Habits

You don't have to replace every bad habit with a high performance habit. In some cases you will be best served by simply eliminating bad habits.

One way to stop yourself from initiating a bad habit is avoiding or eliminating the cue. While this will work, you won't launch into the habit; you really aren't changing or breaking the bad habit.

The golden rule of habit change is, focus on changing only the routine. Don't attempt to change the cue or the reward, substitute a new routine. Use the existing cue and reward to help change the habit.

Select which high performance habits you would like to adopt.

Prioritize these and choose the first one to develop. Write down in detail what adopting this habit is going to do for you. Define explicitly how your life is going to change. Visualize your future with this new habit driving you.

Follow the guidelines on the **Habits Change Process / Change Plan** worksheet. To help make the change process more manageable, remain focused on that one habit at a time and stick to the timing guidelines.

Run a test to see what the new habit routine will feel like. Set a specific start date and determine to implement the new habit routine for thirty, sixty or ninety days. Having a definite start and end date will make the process more manageable and less ominous or threatening; and it will be a process you are more likely to see through.

Chapter 15: Cultivating Habits

Enlist some support. Get some trusted family members and friends to help you throughout your change process. Coach them from the beginning: their role is not to judge but to encourage and support; that is, to help keep you on your new path.

Remember, we are never alone. Your efforts to change can help enhance your relationships. View this – this element of enlisting support – as a habit-development and relationship-building opportunity.

If you plan for success all you have to do is work your plan.

Work it!

Light a fire of motivation and keep it burning. Focus on where you want to go, and maintain that focus. And then take deliberate, consistent action. Develop new habits.

Step by step, habit by habit your routines will change. Your beliefs will change. Your life will change.

It absolutely will!

Now get started developing your plan. We only have a little more ground to cover through a few more chapters before you execute.

Start cultivating new habits now.

Chapter 16
Overcoming What Holds Us Back

Do you believe you are destined for something great?

You are.

The process of adopting high performance habits will accelerate your progress. But as you know, sometimes change is difficult. You have to be ready for challenges. You have to be ready to overcome obstacles. You have to be ready for setbacks. Or, in the case of changing habits, you have to be ready for times when you fall back into old habit patterns.

One obstacle and only one obstacle stands between you and a full and fulfilling life. You must overcome that one obstacle to adopt high performance habits and go where you want to go, do what you want to do, and become the person you are meant to be.

Instead of accepting our "self" as connected, supported, capable and loved; instead of enabling our default setting and living life as a free spirit frolicking in an endlessly creative playground, we too often succumb to the one and only obstacle to ultimate success.

I'll attempt to define this obstacle three different ways.

Chapter 16: Overcoming What Holds Us Back

What I mean in each expression is the same thing. The obstacle blocking the path to success; the hurdle impeding our progress is completely and only internal.

We stumble, we fall, we get beaten up, we get beaten down; whatever it is, we always do it to ourselves.

The one obstacle, the one thing holding us back from a stupendous experience of life, holding us back from performing at an extremely high level, is **lack of faith**.

That may seem like an odd choice of a words, especially since we are talking about developing high performance habits to succeed.

What I mean by lack of faith is that when we struggle, when we resist, when we let fear rule our lives it is because we don't trust life. We do not believe we are connected. We do not believe we are safe. We do not believe we are supported. And we do not believe we are capable. We simply don't believe in life or in ourselves.

Let me present this another way.

The one obstacle holding us back is the core belief we have developed and nurtured about ourselves being alone, at risk, and incapable. These beliefs cause us to protect ourselves at all costs. We must be right. We need to avoid risks. And if we do compete we must dominate.

By our beliefs we confine ourselves to a cell for safe keeping. We cling to what we know.

Chapter 16: Overcoming What Holds Us Back

If judgment, anger, and wrath are emotions you experience regularly, even intermittently, then you have locked yourself in a cage. Judging and getting angry and seeking to punish are strategies of fear. We use these strategies to protect ourselves, protect our status, and protect our self-esteem. These are not the strategies of high performers.

If our beliefs are shallow, fear rules our lives.

We are the unwitting victims of an obstacle we in fact fashion.

Let me attempt to explain this one obstacle in another way.

I'm going to use a word often associated with Sigmund Freud, but my reference here is not meant in the same context. Our one obstacle; the thing holding us back from adopting high performance habits and soaring to new heights is **EGO**.

Ego is the snare of the human condition. Ego implores, berates, condemns the individual to believe he or she is separate from the *Source*, from the environment, and from others.

By placating ego, we invite pain into our lives.

Ego is an unconscious force that, if we let it, will rule our lives and set our core beliefs.

Chapter 16: Overcoming What Holds Us Back

Ego maintains that we are body, and the world, this reality, is what the body can sense. Ego embraces physical reality, dismissing any alternative to what can be seen, touched and manipulated. Ego tells us the world is a dangerous place.

By surrendering to ego, to this belief we are disconnected, limited, weak and alone, we lose contact with our essence, the *Source*. We lose our way.

The tools of ego – the symptoms that manifest from limiting core beliefs, from lack of faith – are **fear** and **resistance to change**.

As you begin to adopt high performance habits beware of these two forces.

Generally, we recognize fear as a negative, disempowering emotion. The energy fear exerts, the impact of fear gripping our bodies, amounts to stress: physical, emotional, and psychological.

Fear is wholly and entirely experienced in the body. We produce, accept, invite in, the emotion of fear by interpreting sensory perceptions; by judging the circumstances we perceive, or by projecting into the future. These mental projections may be inevitable, plausible, or, as is most often the case, entirely imagined.

We broadly distinguish between two types of fear: physical, a threat to the body and or existence; and emotional, a threat to psychological status and or

Chapter 16: Overcoming What Holds Us Back

expectations. A physical fear response is built in. A biochemical process happens in our brains triggering a broader response in our bodies. We can however, dampen or accelerate the energy of fear. Fear is ultimately not from "out there." What we feel; what we know as fear is from within.

Only by truly being at peace in this world can we eliminate fear from our experience. In the meantime, to move in the right direction, act despite fear.

We nurture fear with our intellect and imagination. Only by facing fear, only by stepping outside its influence are we able to expose fear for the deception it is. We must face fear; not to engage fear directly, but rather to recognize it when and where it exists. When we expose fear we lessen its impact. By recognizing, observing fear we dissolve it. Freeing ourselves from the grip of fear we can act.

Acting despite fear is liberating. Make a habit of acting despite fear and fear will lose its influence.

Now on to our other means of self-sabotage.

Life is a kaleidoscope of change; energy in motion. What we perceive as challenges and obstacles come and go. They merge together and they subside. Resistance, clinging, fixes challenges, holds obstacles in place.

We don't grow or advance by freezing our own motion; by clinging tightly to what is. As long as we resist we slow down time and the challenge, the obstacle we confront, stays with us. Really, we stay with it.

Chapter 16: Overcoming What Holds Us Back

High performers succeed changing their circumstances; by being willing to move on.

When facing a challenge many of us have a tendency to dig in, to hold on tight. We cling. We resist the forces of change. Because we are afraid of losing something in the storm of change we batten down the hatches. We attempt to defy the wind. We cling to the rocks in rushing rapids. We focus all our energy on enduring, when the essential activity is to let go.

We advance by growing; by trusting life; by embracing the adventure.

Life is motion, life is change. Yet, for whatever reason we are often averse to change. Too often we resist change, rather than embrace it; even when the change is obviously for our own good.

The tighter we cling to the old the less likely we are to welcome the new.

To overcome the obstacle, the one obstacle to success, we must choose. We must choose to change our habits and change our beliefs.

Choose to let go of beliefs that limit you, that hold you back. Choose to adopt high performance habits and prove to yourself what you are capable of.

Changing your core beliefs is not a cake-walk. It requires work. But, once you unshackle yourself you are free to be, to do, to become.

Chapter 16: Overcoming What Holds Us Back

To overcome limiting beliefs, to build faith instead of fear, to be free of the dominating control of ego, recognize the truth. Confront the brutal facts and choose again.

Once you have made the right choice, once you have opened yourself to the idea that maybe, just maybe, another perspective will serve you better, you release yourself from the grip of what holds you back.

Forgive yourself, your circumstances, and other people. Let go.

Ego need not rule. Don't allow it.

Choose humility and acceptance over the fear, judgment, vengeance and arrogance of ego.

The circumstances of life are neither "someone's" nor "the system's" fault. There is no victim. There is no one to blame. We are not separate; we are masters of our fate.

When we fall victim to fear, or when we cling to current circumstances, we resist life itself.

Great things are ahead of us. Great things are ahead of you. You just need to trust life to take you there.

As you proceed on your high performance habits journey keep this obstacle and its tools of fear and resistance in mind. Set yourself up for success. Plan ways to overcome fear and resistance to change now. Include these strategies in your habit change plan.

Chapter 16: Overcoming What Holds Us Back

Know we each face an obstacle, however we perceive it: as lack of faith, as beliefs about being inadequate and alone in a dangerous world, or as a struggle with ego. Fear and resistance to change are tools we use against ourselves. To change we must take the power away from those tools. We must overcome our fear and resistance to change.

You can overcome fear and resistance to change.

It's okay! You are okay!

Grow bigger than the one obstacle you face; the one you hold inside.

We have one more chapter before we jump into the change process in earnest. In that chapter we are going to focus on leadership. We know we do not survive alone and we do not succeed alone. High performers cooperate and collaborate to break new ground.

Going new places, overcoming challenges, and holding the team together is the work of leaders; a position high performers often find themselves in.

As you overcome the obstacle that holds you back you will naturally become a leader. Lead with integrity. Lead from the front. Establish the right leadership habits from the start.

Chapter 17
Leading by Example

Are you a leader?

Do you aspire to be one?

In this chapter we devote our attention to leadership.

You may be wondering why we are talking about leadership in a program about high performance habits.

If you have stuck with me this far, you understand relationships are a fundamental aspect, the fundamental aspect of success. Selecting, nurturing, and contributing to life enhancing relationships constitutes success in life.

Typically, mostly, usually, as we conduct our lives, across every area and dimension, we fill one of two roles: we follow or we lead.

Every exchange between two human beings is a leadership opportunity. It is an opportunity to influence another or be influenced by them.

If you are a parent, you must lead.

If people work for you as employees or provide you services directly, you potentially are a leader.

If people look to you for guidance and insight, if you influence other people, you are a leader.

In every engagement you are potentially a leader.

Chapter 17: Leading by Example

Understanding how to lead is a critical component of developing high performance habits. To effectively remake yourself, to manage your journey, to ensure your success, you simply must lead.

Because most people settle for getting by and determine to react to circumstances rather than define them, high performing people naturally rise to the top as leaders. High performing people are going places, doing things, making things happen. People naturally look to high performers for positive inspiration.

Right from the start here though, I must make a distinction. When I talk about being a leader, about leading and about leadership, I'm not talking about engagement through formal and informal power structures.

Typically, usually, mostly, people tend to equate leading and leadership with position and power. People put themselves into positions of relative power, where someone in a high power position has the ability to give or take from the person in the lower power position. The powerful person can inflict punishment or offer reward to influence, determine or manipulate behavior.

The exercise of power is often confused with leadership. This is not what I am talking about.

Leadership, in a word is inspiration.

The single defining characteristic of a leader, any leader, good or otherwise, is inspiration. A leader inspires people.

Chapter 17: Leading by Example

A leader stirs people. A leader, through word and deed, causes people to move, to act, to create or destroy. A leader ignites desire, whether to realize pleasure or avoid pain, and gets people to do things they otherwise would not do.

To inspire action, a leader provides either one or both of the indispensable and invaluable assets required to achieve any purpose: vision and motivation.

Leaders spend their time, energy and talents creating and sharing relevant visions of worthwhile objectives. And leaders provide the energy, the drive, and the discipline to move the team forward toward the goal. Teams fail when leaders fail to inspire.

Every inspirational leader possesses two essential qualities: caring and competence. Leadership is about a leader knowing what he or she is doing; being technically competent at the task at hand; and genuinely caring about people.

If a leader is not competent succeeding at a task then falls to, and depends on, the team members. If the leader is competent but doesn't care about people the team may achieve the objective, but that leader is not a success. Leadership is about connecting people and creating value collectively.

Good leaders are tenacious, intelligent, and caring. They have developed and consistently maintain high performance habits.

Chapter 17: Leading by Example

Good leaders promote worthwhile goals and seek the common good.

Achievement depends on choices leaders make.

Being a great leader is a lonely calling. Knowing the right thing to do is hard enough; doing it is sometimes next to impossible. But that is what great leaders do: make the impossible possible.

You have the potential to lead in every interaction you have with another human being.

Sometimes you should lead. Sometimes you should follow. Sometimes you must lead. Sometimes you must follow.

What do I mean by that?

Even the highest performers among us are not immune to life's trials and tribulations. Sometimes, and if we develop high performance habits that's most of the time, we bring a positive attitude and growth mindset to interpersonal exchanges. By our competent, respectful and enthusiastic demeanor we raise the energy of the people we engage.

At other times, when our batteries are running low, we depend on the inspiration, the vision and motivation of others to set us on the right course.

In common social exchanges, a positive attitude and growth mindset will enhance every engagement. With wisdom and experience we come to recognize when to lead and when to follow.

Chapter 17: Leading by Example

Sometimes we provide the inspiration. Sometimes we absorb the inspiration. That is why we are all here; to help each other.

As a leader in a formal role, say as a parent or a boss, you are challenged to make hard choices.

This power dynamic I alluded to earlier is an all too common factor in human relations. And we must be very cognizant of and careful with this dynamic.

Everyone is on their own path, making their own way, conducting their life journey. We all are charged to do the best we can with what we've got. We help others. Others help us. But we do not live the others' lives. We can help people up, but we cannot carry them to their final destination. Remember this.

Keep yourself straight. Keep yourself energized. Develop and nurture high performance habits and you will inspire other people. They in turn will advance. This is how life works.

Most people do not understand, accept or believe they have absolute power over their lives so they conduct their lives, they live, always forfeiting or giving away their power. They unknowingly become victims of circumstance; susceptible to the whims, the dictates, the influence of others.

Victims usually come to regret their lack of power and settle into a negative, fixed mindset. Once they have the negativity turned on, every engagement reflects the negative

Chapter 17: Leading by Example

energy they project. Their energy reflects back to its source: them.

So, be aware, be prepared. Like facing fear you must be ready to manage power others abdicate.

Do not claim that power, as power truly does corrupt. But manage it and move forward.

As a growth minded leader your best strategy is to provide positive energy to every situation. At the same time you must not allow negative energy to impact you. As the opportunity demands, or allows, help negative minded individuals recognize they are not powerless. Inspire them to assume responsibility. Inspire them to change course and get moving in the right direction.

Do not knowingly or unwittingly forfeit your personal power. High performers understand they control their own response to life. And high performers know it is by trial and tribulation that human beings strengthen themselves; effort before reward.

High performers are willing to put forth effort to progress.

Effective, inspiring leaders, high performers, bear the burden of personal responsibility. Running from adversity only offers regrets, never victory.

An individual's success, a family's success, a team's success, a business's success, a nation's success depends on leadership.

Chapter 17: Leading by Example

Leadership is the intangible quality that inspires people to advance.

Leadership gets people to focus on a worthwhile objective and leadership provides the energy to keep people advancing despite hardships and challenges.

In an ideal world, in an ideal family or an ideal organization every individual understands and is committed to the best objective; the goal that advances their interests and the interests of all other people. But in the real world, most people do not recognize worthwhile objectives on their own. Someone else raises their sights, opens the door, blazes the path. These are high performing leaders.

A leader inspires by offering vision and fueling action.

Lead by nurturing people's internal energy of desire; their drive. Lead by crafting, creating or revealing a worthy goal and stirring the resolve to act.

Inspire. Provide a worthwhile vision and a positive example. Inspire with persistent encouragement and keep people moving toward that vision.

While most people consider being in a superior position or possessing formal or informal authority as the equivalent of leading, you know this just isn't so.

When talking about good and bad leaders we hone in on certain attributes and characteristics. We point out leaders as people possessing things like confidence and strength; and the ability to direct others. We think of leaders as people who direct others to do things; tell people what to do. We

Chapter 17: Leading by Example

often fall back to an authoritarian model of leadership. The authoritarian model misses the essence of leadership.

Ultimately every individual is responsible for his or her own actions. Leadership facilitates progress. Leadership inspires action.

Here is a way to determine whether you are leading or being led.

Characterize your encounter with another person, this potential leadership interaction, by means of two simple gestures.

If the action to be completed comes down to a direction (as if pointing) you are not being led. Or if you are the one directing someone else, in a way that is akin to pointing, you are not leading.

Call the interaction what you will: informing, educating, enlightening; activities that pass on insight or information; or call it: coercion, compulsion, intimidation, direction, pressuring, command or control. These are power methods; influence applied with a threat of punishment or loss. These tactics are not leading, they are not leadership.

If the engagement comes down to pointing someone on their way, the engagement is not leadership.

Leadership is always expressed another way, by means of another gesture; a gesture you are familiar with. It's that sign of calling someone over; of motioning another to come along. It's a signal saying, "Come with me; I will show the way."

Chapter 17: Leading by Example

A leader takes the lead. A leader advances at the front. A leader moves deliberately toward a valuable destination.

A leader, by their advance, inspires others to move forward; to aspire to something more, to something worthwhile; to do more, to become more.

My definition of leadership is not mainstream.

In my definition, real leadership is always about achieving something beneficial, something worthwhile; creating value. Leadership is never self-serving or selfish.

Real leadership is selfless in that by fulfilling a purpose, by moving toward some worthwhile end that leader leads. He or she inspires others to be, to do, to become more.

Leaders do not point and declare or direct.

Leaders through their actions, through their words and most importantly through their deeds, inspire others to follow.

Leaders inspire people to go where they would not have gone were it not for the inspiration of a worthy example.

Leadership does not divide, it connects. Leadership does not distinguish between haves and have not's. Leadership is the act of advancing and by advancing fearlessly inspiring others to follow.

"Come with me; let me show you the way." This is leadership.

Remember this distinction the next time you are in a position to lead.

Chapter 17: Leading by Example

People will follow when they know you care about them and they trust you to help them get to a better destination.

People will follow you anywhere when they know you will endure the hardships along the way and share the weight of the load.

Lead by gesturing people to follow. Lead by example, not by pointing them on their way.

We are nearly at the end of our journey together.

I hope you recognize that you have the ability to be a significant influence in this world.

The world needs good leaders. People need worthy examples to emulate.

By developing high performance habits you will become a conduit for the energy of life to flow and grow.

You can do this. You can lead.

You can have more, do more, and become more.

Set your sights high. Establish a worthwhile goal.

And take one step at a time.

Habit by habit, as you eliminate habits that do not serve you and replace them with habits that do, your life will change.

We are moving into our concluding chapters. Next we look back at the ground we have covered on this ***High Performance Habits*** journey.

Chapter 18
Change Your Habits, Change Your Life

At this point in ***High Performance Habits*** a sense of relief and a sense of accomplishment are both appropriate.

We have traveled a long way together.

I hope you are anxious and excited to proceed. As you know the work is just beginning.

You would not be working through a program like this unless you have an intention to grow and a belief that you can grow; a belief that you can have more, do more and be more.

And, yes, you really can.

Over the course of these four parts we examined the lives of four extraordinary people. I say extraordinary not because of who those people are or were, but because of what they did.

Every person has the capability to do extraordinary things.

You have the ability to do extraordinary things.

You can become a successful business person and wealthy philanthropist like Andrew Carnegie. You can create and invent like Thomas Edison. You can connect with people across the country and around the world and build a network inspiring millions like Oprah Winfrey. And you can walk by faith, overcoming obstacles, and sharing a message

Chapter 18: Change Your Habits, Change Your Life

of hope with people young and old; people you encounter along the way, like Bill Irwin.

Everyone has extraordinary potential. Everyone has access to unlimited wisdom and power. It's a pity so few seek to fulfill their potential. It's a pity so few embrace the adventure and leverage all they have access to.

The difference between the high achievers, the super-successful and all the rest is not looks or talent, intelligence or education, and access to resources and wealth. The difference between high-fliers and the just-getting-byers is the willingness to adopt high performance habits.

It takes effort, it takes vision, and it takes determination to develop high performance habits. Change is not always easy, but it is always possible. Change is the nature of life. Problems arise when we resist change or when we move in the wrong direction.

You can start moving in the right direction. You can be so much more.

If you make your habits work for you instead of against you, you will go farther, faster, and there is no telling what magnificence you can manifest.

You are here to create, to grow, to add value to life. If you do that, you cannot help but succeed.

The quality and the achievements of our lives rest on our connection with the *Source*. This connection is defined by

Chapter 18: Change Your Habits, Change Your Life

our core beliefs: what we believe about this world, ourselves, and our place in this world.

The foundation of our lives is built on this connection – on our core beliefs.

If we believe we are connected, competent and loved and that we have a reason for being in this world, a contribution to make, we embrace the adventure. We build on a solid foundation. We nurture a positive attitude and a growth mindset. This makes all things possible.

If we believe we are lost and alone, adrift in a dangerous world with only our wits and talents to rely on, we are in for a long, hard slog.

We can define the difference in these two sets of beliefs with a few simple words. The implications, however, for lives lived by people subscribing to one or the other of these beliefs is immense.

What do you think?

You have examined your core beliefs. Must they change?

We talked about the power of focus.

The *Pareto Principle* or the *80/20 Rule* reminds us that only a few things really matter. If we want to go far in life, if we want to do great things, we should focus on those few things that really, really matter.

Chapter 18: Change Your Habits, Change Your Life

We need to apply our time, energy and effort to the biggest levers we can find. With a large enough lever we can move the world.

Habits, high performance habits are just such levers.

Early on we dissected the habit loop. You will recall the four parts of the cycle: the cue or trigger; the craving; the routine; and the reward.

We empower habits in our lives as an energy conservation measure. We implement a routine frequently enough that we eliminate conscious thought from the process. This saves us effort. We take thought out of the equation. We move from cue, which stirs a craving, through routine, to reward automatically.

The difficulty with habits arise when our habits hinder our progress instead of enhance it.

You conducted your own habits inventory, perhaps with the aid of family, friends and or co-workers. You likely now have a somewhat comprehensive list of the things you do habitually, good and bad.

We have to confront the brutal facts so as to inform our decisions on what we should do and which way we should go.

Working with our **Habits Inventory** we were able to determine which habits are not serving us – which habits must go.

Chapter 18: Change Your Habits, Change Your Life

Reflecting on the lives of the high achievers we discussed in **High Performance Habits** and looking at the lives of the high performers we see in society around us, we recognize a few key traits and characteristics which these people make habits. It is these habits, these high performance habits driving their success.

Carnegie, Edison, Oprah and Irwin all focused on learning and growth. They had positive attitudes and growth mindsets. All of them were willing to take risks. All of them would routinely go the extra mile, doing more than just what was necessary. And all of them built and relied on a support network to see them through. They were positive, perceptive and persistent.

They did not have it easy. They were not lucky; they had significant challenges to overcome. They just kept moving forward. They kept giving of themselves and in the end they realized astonishing achievement.

This is exactly what we have to do.

Turn to that list of high performance habits (Appendix A). It is not an endless list. The list consists of those levers, those habits that deliver the biggest impact.

Attitude and Mindset.

Confidence, fitness and health.

Building a network of positive, supportive people.

Communicating to connect and empower.

Chapter 18: Change Your Habits, Change Your Life

We do not have to do everything. And it is best that we do not try to change everything all at once. It is a matter of doing the best we can with what we've got. Step by step, habit by habit we can change.

You have your **Habits Change Plan**.

Set your timeline. Construct your plan, and then work you plan.

The biggest hurdles to overcome, really the only hurdles to overcome, are internal. Your terror barrier is fixed in place attempting to protect your core beliefs.

Fear and resistance to change are the tools you use against yourself.

Face them down. Just by exposing your fear, recognizing fear for what it is, will reduce fear's influence. Fear grows in the dark, but withers under the light. Turn on the light.

As you begin the habits change process you are going to run into cultural resistance. You've been party to group habits that have formed in your family, at work, in every group you associate with. Enlist support from people you trust to help you through this change process. Habit by habit step by step keep moving forward.

By intending to become a high performer you are taking on the role and responsibility of a leader. By your efforts and intentions you inspire others.

Chapter 18: Change Your Habits, Change Your Life

See the task through.

Your high performance habits will inspire those you love and may even cause those you encounter to see life from a new perspective. You just might possibly move others to take action and initiate some worthwhile changes of their own.

With high performance habits the sky is the limit.

I am anxious to see you soar.

One last thing.

My intent with **High Performance Habits** is to give you something of value. I hope I have achieved that, but I know this book and the audio-visual program can be tweaked and improved.

Please let me know what you think of the ideas presented in this program, **High Performance Habits**, and please share with me your suggestions for improvement. I have included an example of a feedback sheet and my contact information in Appendix C.

With your help I can take this program the extra mile and together we can inspire countless others to live extraordinary lives.

Most people don't complete a book or program they begin. Thank you for making this journey with me. It's been my honor and privilege to share my life with you.

Chapter 18: Change Your Habits, Change Your Life

Our journey together is not quite over. We have explored some ideas, we have examined, we have considered, we have compiled, and we have planned.

It is time now to act. One more chapter to go.

Chapter 19
Take the Next Step

Guess what?

It's time.

It is time to take action. It is time to act.

It is time to implement your plan.

It is time to break some bad habits and in their place install some new high performance habits.

It is time to begin the work in earnest of reshaping yourself and reorienting the course of your life journey.

If you have stuck with **_High Performance Habits_**; if you have worked through the entire program you have been subtly changing your mindset. You have come to believe that change is possible. You have hope for a brighter future and you have developed a strategy for moving forward.

Just like there is no such thing as passive listening, we are either listening actively or we are not listening, there is no such thing as passive faith.

You see faith is only and always active.

What you do, the actions you take are a reflection of, are a demonstration of, your faith. What you believe is what you live by.

Chapter 19: Take the Next Step

Every individual that wanders lost; every life that wallows in mediocrity; every human being that struggles to discern which way to go or even to go at all is dealing with a crisis of faith. The habits they adopt are strategies that reflect that faith, those core beliefs, good, bad, or indifferent.

We can only succeed by attempting.

The prize is out there. That prize is waiting – it's waiting for you to claim it. Your life can be so much more.

We succeed only when we put forth effort.

We succeed only when we move forward, when we advance.

Waiting for conditions to be just right; waiting for the stars to align; waiting for some events to unfold is an excuse, an excuse driven by fear.

Make success a habit. Act. Move forward. Advance.

There is no other way to go.

Life isn't going to wait for you. Life is calling out for you to join the fun.

Make it happen.

You can. Yes, you can!

Take out your plan.

Your ultimate objective is to put your life on the fast track to the success and achievement you know you are capable of realizing. You know you have an automatic pilot;

Chapter 19: Take the Next Step

your built-in habit forming tendency. You just have to reprogram that automatic pilot. Reprogram that automatic pilot with habits that accelerate your progress – high performance habits.

Remember, we never totally eliminate old habit patterns. But we want to make new habits, new high performance habits, that stick.

So think of your strategy as climbing a ladder.

You take one step at a time; one habit at a time.

Choose the habit to replace. Sketch out the habit cycle. Identify the cue, the craving, the routine and the reward. Test out a new routine. Then test it again. Establish a habit change timeline with a specific start date and running time, thirty days, sixty days, ninety days or something in between. Enlist some support from people you can trust.

Have you done all that?

Now execute. Enact the plan. Act.

Just by doing something you empower your faith. Your faith will grow. Your beliefs will change.

A new life is possible. Don't dream about it. Do something about it.

Once you have successfully adopted a new habit routine take the next step up the ladder.

Chapter 19: Take the Next Step

Think of making your way, of advancing through this change process, as climbing that ladder. Start off with easy tasks, easy habit routines. You won't be far off the ground. It's not too scary. As you progress and work on breaking more powerful bad habits and adopting high performance habits you will begin to get excited by the new view, the new perspective you gain from climbing that ladder.

Every success, every habit routine you change, is evidence to fuel your faith.

You can change. You can become a high performer. No one is holding you back.

Take another step up the ladder.

Your perspective will change each rung higher you climb. You will start to see things differently in all areas of your life. Keep going.

If you started small, your habits change sequence should proceed toward implementing, embracing, a high performance habit: a positive attitude, a growth mindset, health and fitness, building an interconnected support network, or developing effective, relationship-enhancing communication skills.

Once you have developed one of these high leverage habits, work the lever and keep going.

This change process, step by step, habit by habit, is the process of reprogramming your automatic pilot – of changing your core beliefs.

Chapter 19: Take the Next Step

You are flipping the switches back to operating on your default setting; that setting that intended a life of adventure, a life of love, and a life of joy.

You are on a high performance journey.

Keep going.

Change your habits. Adopt and nurture high performance habits.

Become the person you are meant to become.

The light you fuel, the bright glow of your flame, is not just to light your path. The light you shine lights the way for all those people around you.

You are a light for the world.

Let your light shine!

HIGH PERFORMANCE HABITS

HIGH PERFORMANCE HABITS

Afterword

There you have it. It's really quite simple. Habits dominate our lives for good or bad. Our habits, the things we do automatically, without thinking, set us up for success or failure. The men and women who travel the farthest, the fastest; the men and women who do the most, experience the most, and achieve the most – high performers – develop and employ high performance habits. You can too.

You can be a high achiever, a high performer. You can go farther, faster. You can have more, do more and be more. You just have to start pulling the right levers. You have to eliminate the habits that hurt you; the habits that hold you back. You have to start nurturing and developing habits that accelerate your progress; habits the move you forward, that carry you to new heights.

Hopefully you see that now. Hopefully you recognize you have talents and abilities, you have skills you have not yet explored or exploited. You can do so much more. Stop wasting your time and energy doing thoughtless things, things that don't serve you, that don't advance your cause. Instead of empowering bad habit processes, instead of chaining yourself to mediocrity, unleash your potential. Deliberately change those habits that don't serve you into high performance habits and soar like an eagle.

Take advantage of your natural programming, of human nature. Program your automatic pilot to take you to exciting places, exhilarating places, and keep moving forward. Once you make success a habit an extraordinary life will unfold. You are guaranteed to succeed!

Words are a poor substitute for communicating what is best expressed through the actions of example. You are left now to go out and test these ideas in the real world – in the laboratory, the playground that is life – just like I'm doing. If you experiment with an open mind your perspective will broaden, your attitude will change and your faith will deepen. Once you have enough faith you can move mountains. Great things are in store for you. Believe!

Scott F. Paradis

Appendix A
High Performance Habits Summary List

People who consistently perform at a high level; people who travel far and travel fast; people who produce something of value, achieve much, and experience a great adventure on this journey of life develop and nurture high performance habits. They make success a habit. By developing high performance habits you can too.

KEYSTONE OR LEVER HABITS

- ❖ Connect with *Source* (meditates, prays – values based)
- ❖ Positive Attitude (grateful, open, accepting, excited and enthusiastic about life)
- ❖ Growth Mindset (develops self, always learning, seeks out challenges and opportunities, willing to take risks, willing to struggle and fail)
- ❖ Action / Goal Oriented (cultivates worthwhile, challenging vision, focuses on objectives, keeps moving forward)
- ❖ Physically Active / Exercises (healthy, fit and engaged)
- ❖ Develop Communication and Leadership Skills (works consistently and deliberately to enhance social skills)
- ❖ Build and Maintain a Robust Support Network (associates with, supports and draws support from like-minded, positive people)
- ❖ Create / Produce (contributes value to other people and the world – adds to life)

Employing these habits reinforces productive core beliefs. People who embrace life using *Lever Habits* are competent, capable, confident and persistent. They are high performers.

Appendix B
High Performance Habits Change Process / Change Plan

We human beings are creatures of habit. We rely on habits to simplify our lives. Habits either help us fulfill our potential or hinder our progress. To become all we have the potential to be we must choose, develop and nurture the right habits.

Making a change requires three elements: motivation, a new focus, and a willingness to act. Habits, however, are routines we build and reinforce over time. Each individual habit is governed by a cue and a coveted reward. To deliberately change our habits we will employ a deliberate change process.

DELIBERATE HABITS CHANGE PROCESS

1. Assess Your Habits: evaluate each habit to determine if it hurts or helps.

2. Prioritize Habits to Change: determine where to start.

3. Identify Habit Cycle Elements: sketch out habit cycle (cue > craving > routine > reward) for those habits that must change.

4. Select New Habits to Adopt: develop a new vision.

5. Make a Plan: include the "big picture" and implementation details.

6. Test: run through the new habit routine a few times; adjust plan.

7. Enlist Support: get help from people you can count on and trust.

8. Execute: implement the plan, change a habit; adjust plan; keep going.

Step 1: Assess your habits
- Complete your **Habits Inventory**.
- Evaluate each of your habits (+ positive, - negative, / neutral) to determine which habits must change.
- Highlight, on your **Habits Inventory**, those habits you intend to eliminate or replace.

Step 2: Prioritize the habits to change.
- Review you **Habits Inventory**.
- Create a prioritized list of habits you are going to eliminate. Start this list with the first habit (#1) to replace and continue with the second habit (#2) and so on.

Step 3: Produce a Habit Cycle sketch for the habit you intend to change.

- Sketch out the **Habit Cycle** for the habit you intend to change.
- Identify the "Cue" / "Trigger" (the stimulus which initiates the habit cycle).
- Identify the "Craving" / "Desire" (the feeling the cue or trigger initiates).
- Describe the "Routine" (the state or mood (for a feeling habit cycle) or the thought pattern (for a thinking habit cycle) or the action sequence (for an action habit cycle) that is the heart of the habit process).
- Identify the "Reward" (that something you get at the end of the habit cycle; ultimately this is a feeling).

Carefully conduct this detective work. The routine part of the habit cycle is the easiest part to identify. The Cue, the Craving, and the Reward are not necessarily easy to determine. Take some time to identify the true motive. Do not assume you are eating because you are hungry. The real reason may be that you are lonely or tired or upset or up against a challenging obstacle. Dig into each component of the habit cycle and discuss the process with someone you trust to help sort it out.

Step 4: Select a new routine or habit to replace the old habit that does not serve you.

- Select new habits to adopt. Specify the new routine, the new habit that you are going to adapt in place of the old habit.
- Test the new routine. How does it feel? Does the new routine generate a positive outcome? Describe the outcome in detail.
- Write out a vision statement for this new habit. What will life be like once you adopt the new habit routine? What are you intending to achieve? Focus on and stress "WHY"; that is what is motivating about this change.
- Build toward adopting high performance lever habits.

Step 5: Develop the specific change plan.

- You have identified the habit to change and sketched out the Habit Cycle for that habit. You have selected a new routine, tested it, and envisioned a new you after adopting the routine. You have a clear goal and vision statement written out.
- Select a new habit implementation start date (when you are going to start).
- Specify the length of time you will focus on adopting the new habit routine. This could range from one week to 90 days.
- Think through and write down what you are going to do when you relapse; that is when you fall into your old

habit routine. This is a means of starting again, not abandoning the effort.
- Determine who specifically you are going to enlist to help you through this change process.

Step 6: Run another test. Get familiar with the new habit routine. Believe you can change.

Step 7: Enlist support. Get your family members, friends and coworkers on board.

Step 8: Execute. Implement the plan.

Once you succeed with one habit move on to the next one and keep going. It is like climbing a ladder one rung at a time.

Step by step, habit by habit, you are going to create a new you; a new life.

Appendix C
Feedback Request and Contact Information

You have put a lot of time, energy and effort working through this program. You have a unique perspective to offer. So that we can improve the content, the presentation and, most importantly, the results of this program please provide your feedback on the strengths and weakness of ***High Performance Habits***.

Please send me, Scott F. Paradis, an email with your thoughts.

Here are some questions for you to consider that might help you formulate some feedback, but please don't feel constrained by this list:

- What did you like LEAST about ***High Performance Habits***?
- Was ***High Performance Habits*** worth your time? Yes or No. Why?
- Which idea, chapter or part did you most enjoy or find most useful / helpful? Why?
- Would you recommend ***High Performance Habits*** to others? Yes or No. Why?
- What can we include or improve to enhance the implementation or change process component of the ***High Performance Habits*** program?

Send the email to Scott@c-achieve.com

If you would like me to speak to your group about ***High Performance Habits*** or another **Success 101 Workshop** offering, or if I can help you in some way, please call and leave a voice mail at:

(703) 772-3521

Be sure to leave contact information and I will get back to you as soon as possible.

Thank you!

About the Author

Scott F. Paradis is a student of life and a seeker of ultimate truth. Striving to simplify the complex he studies human performance and potential through the disciplines of economics, business, human relations, communications, politics, philosophy, religion, athletics, and health and fitness to discern simple truths: the wisdom of life. Only once something is made simple can we, do we, truly understand.

A native of New Hampshire, as of this writing Scott lives in northern Virginia where he concluded a 30-year career with the United States Army. He is married to a shining star, the former Lisa Newcombe, and has two extraordinary adult children: Merideth and Mitchell.

Leading by example Scott helps people live full and fulfilling lives in this extraordinary reality. He helps people dream big and build faith by establishing life-affirming habits of thinking, feeling and acting. And he helps people relate to others and life in positive, fulfilling ways.

Scott retired from the Army at the rank of colonel. In addition to varied stateside assignments he completed tours in Europe and the Middle East. He served as a National Security Fellow with the John F. Kennedy School of Government at Harvard University and as a National Defense Congressional Fellow with the United States Senate. He holds a Master of Science in Administration from Central Michigan University and a Bachelor of Arts in Sociology from the University of New Hampshire.

Scott's personal aspiration is for his life to be a message of hope, an example of faith, and an expression of love as he works to do the best he can with what he's got.

Acknowledgements

Everything I have done, everything I do, and everything I am yet to accomplish is made possible by the loving and supportive people that surround me and by those that are drawn into my awareness. It is the inspiration of the *Source* and the genius and generosity of other people that make my success possible.

For Lisa, my wife, and my two terrific children, Merideth and Mitchell, my sister Renee and all my family and friends I am forever grateful. I am truly blessed having wonderful people in my life.

To past sages and modern day prophets expressing truth through insightful words and faithful examples I extend my most heartfelt thanks. The courage, commitment and sacrifice of men and women who embrace the opportunity that is life inspire me. I pray that the words etched on these pages might inspire you to take on laudable challenges, endure worthwhile hardships, and fulfill what I know to be limitless potential.

Success101Workshop.com

Success 101 Workshop is all about improving **performance** and helping people **live life to the fullest**. In our inspiring presentations and engaging workshops we focus on the fundamentals while striving to simplify the seemingly complex.

If you want to learn a task, if you want to improve, if you want to master something, focus on the fundamentals. Once you master the fundamentals there's no stopping you.

Through consultations, presentations and workshops, online courses and published insights ***Success 101 Workshop*** shows individuals how to live exhilarating lives of outstanding achievement and helps teams succeed beyond expectations.

We throw open the curtains obscuring simple truths. We help people see things the way they are and then imagine how great things could be. Then we set them on a new course.

Success, in business and in life, is not a matter of commanding irresistible power and employing overwhelming resources, it is a matter of doing the best you can with what you've got. You have more assets at your disposal than you know. By relying on your natural abilities and learning and leveraging the fundamental principles of success you can change your body, your mind, your business: your life. Yes you really can!

You have potential you haven't yet begun to tap. Contact us now, we can help.

Available from:
Scott F. Paradis
Success101Workshop
Success 101 Workshop.com
&
Cornerstone Achievements

Books:

High Performance Habits
Making Success a Habit

How to Succeed at Anything
In 3 Simple Steps

Success 101 How Life Works
Know the Rules, Play to Win

Promise and Potential
A Life of Wisdom, Courage, Strength and Will

Warriors Diplomats Heroes, Why America's Army Succeeds
Lessons for Business and Life

Look for these online courses offered by Scott F. Paradis:

High Performance Habits, Making Success a Habit
Success 101 How to Succeed, Focus on Fundamentals
High Performance Health and Fitness, MNOP Habits
Money, The New Science of Making It

More online courses offered by Scott F. Paradis:

Success 101 How Life Works, Know the Rules, Play to Win
High Performance Leadership, Fundamental Leadership Habits
Loving 101, Making Love a Habit
Achievement Theology, Bringing the Wisdom of the Ages to Life

Contact us to schedule a presentation, a consultation or a performance oriented workshop:

High Performance Habits, Making Success a Habit
Success 101 How to Succeed, Focus on Fundamentals
High Performance Leadership, Fundamental Leadership Habits
Money, The New Science of Making It

www.ingramcontent.com/pod-product-compliance
Lightning Source LLC
Chambersburg PA
CBHW071416160426
43195CB00013B/1711